"Information through Innovation"

Contributors

The Publisher would like to express great appreciation to those individuals that contributed to the overall development of the STAR Series.

Joseph Dennin
Fairfield University

Edward Harms
Interactive Business Systems, Inc.

Philip J. Judd
Napier & Judd, Inc.

H. Albert Napier
Rice University

Kathleen Stewart
Moraine Valley Community College

Patrice Gapen
Laramie County Community College

Mary Last
Grand Valley State University

Patricia McMahon
Moraine Valley Community College

Philip J. Pratt
Grand Valley State University

Star

WordPerfect 5.1

Kathleen Stewart
Moraine Valley
Community College

Patricia McMahon
Moraine Valley
Community College

A volume in the Boyd & Fraser STAR Series

boyd & fraser publishing company

Credits:

Publisher: Thomas K. Walker
Acquisitions Editor: James H. Edwards
Production Coordinator: Pat Stephan
Manufacturing Coordinator: Dean Sherman
Composition: Gex, Inc.
Cover Design: Hannus Design, Inc.

boyd & fraser

A Division of South-Western Publishing Company
Danvers, MA 01923

Manufactured in the United States of America.

The Star Series is printed on recycled, acid-free paper that meets Environmental Protection Agency standards.

ISBN: 0-87835-734-3

2 3 4 5 6 7 8 9 10 DH 5 4 3

Brief Table of Contents

TOPIC 1 *Getting Started* 3

TOPIC 2 *Creating and Saving a New Document* 9

TOPIC 3 *Revising and Resaving a Document* 15

TOPIC 4 *Printing a Document* 25

TOPIC 5 *Setting and Changing Margins* 31

TOPIC 6 *Setting and Changing Tabs* 41

TOPIC 7 *Changing Line Spacing and Paper Orientation* 49

Checkpoint 1 55

TOPIC 8 *Changing the Appearance of Text* 59

TOPIC 9 *Using Blocks of Text* 67

TOPIC 10 *Moving and Copying Text* 75

TOPIC 11 *Aligning Text* 83

TOPIC 12 *Searching and Replacing* 93

TOPIC 13 *Using Spell and the Thesaurus* 101

TOPIC 14 *Managing Files* 109

Checkpoint 2 115

TOPIC 15 *Controlling Page Endings* 119

TOPIC 16 *Using Page Numbers* 129

TOPIC 17 *Using Headers and Footers* 137

TOPIC 18 *Using Footnotes* 145

TOPIC 19 *Preparing Form Letters* 153

TOPIC 20 *Printing Envelopes* 163

Checkpoint 3 171

Contents

Editor's Foreword xi

Introduction to Word Processing 1

TOPIC 1 *Getting Started* 3

Starting WordPerfect 5.1 3
The Document Edit Screen 3
Using Menus 4
Using Keyboard Commands 4
Checking the Current Directory 4
Using Help 4
Exiting WordPerfect 4
Tutorial 4 • Exercise 8

TOPIC 2 *Creating and Saving a New Document* 9

Typing Text 9
Moving the Cursor 9
Saving the Document 10
Clearing the Screen 10
Tutorial 11 • Exercises 14

TOPIC 3 *Revising and Resaving a Document* 15

Retrieving a File 15
Listing Files 15
Inserting Text 15
Deleting Text 16
Undeleting Text 16
Resaving a File 16
Tutorial 16 • Exercises 23

TOPIC 4 *Printing a Document* 25

Previewing a Document 25
Printing a Page 25
Printing from the List 25
Canceling a Print Job 26
Tutorial 26 • Exercises 30

TOPIC 5 *Setting and Changing Margins* 31

Setting Left and Right Margins 31
Setting Top and Bottom Margins 31
Changing Margins 31
Deleting a Code 32
Inserting a Code 32
Tutorial 32 • Exercises 40

TOPIC 6 *Setting and Changing Tabs* 41

Setting Tabs 41
Changing Tabs 41
Using Different Tab Types 41
Tutorial 42 • Exercises 48

TOPIC 7 *Changing Line Spacing and Paper Orientation* 49

Changing the Line Spacing 49
Changing the Paper Orientation 49
Tutorial 50 • Exercises 53

Checkpoint 1 55

What You Should Know 55
Review Questions 55
Checkpoint Problems 56

TOPIC 8 *Changing the Appearance of Text* 59

Using Underline or Bold 59
Using Italic or Other Styles 59
Using Fonts 60
Tutorial 60 • Exercises 66

TOPIC 9 *Using Blocks of Text* 67

Defining a Block of Text 67
Deleting a Block 67
Saving a Block 67
Printing a Block 68
Tutorial 68 • Exercises 73

TOPIC 10 *Moving and Copying Text* 75

Moving Text 75
Copying Text 75
Appending Text 75
Tutorial 76 • Exercises 81

TOPIC 11 *Aligning Text* 83

Centering Text Horizontally 83
Centering Text Vertically 83
Justifying Text 83
Right-Aligning Text 84
Using Indents 84
Tutorial 85 • Exercises 91

TOPIC 12 *Searching and Replacing* 93

Searching for Text or Codes 93
Searching and Replacing Text 93
Tutorial 94 • Exercises 99

TOPIC 13 *Using Spell and the Thesaurus* 101

Checking the Spelling 101
Using the Thesaurus 102
Tutorial 102 • Exercises 107

TOPIC 14 *Managing Files* 109

Deleting a File 109
Copying a File 109
Renaming a File 109
Finding a File 110
Tutorial 110 • Exercises 114

Checkpoint 2 115

What You Should Know 115
Review Questions 115
Checkpoint Problems 116

TOPIC 15 *Controlling Page Endings* 119

Using Soft Page Breaks 119
Keeping Lines Together on a Page 119
Using Widow/Orphan Protection 119
Using a Hard Page Break 120
Tutorial 120 • Exercises 127

TOPIC 16 *Using Page Numbers* 129

Starting Page Numbers 129
Changing the Page Number 129
Choosing a Page Number Position 129
Stopping the Page Numbers 130
Tutorial 130 • Exercises 135

TOPIC 17 *Using Headers and Footers* 137

Creating a Header or Footer 137
Editing a Header or Footer 137
Suppressing a Header or Footer 138
Tutorial 138 • Exercises 143

TOPIC 18 *Using Footnotes* 145

Creating a Footnote 145
Editing a Footnote 145
Deleting a Footnote 145
Moving a Footnote 146
Tutorial 146 • Exercises 152

TOPIC 19 *Preparing Form Letters* 153

Creating a Primary File 153
Creating a Secondary File 154
Printing Merge Letters 155
Tutorial 155 • Exercises 160

TOPIC 20 *Printing Envelopes* 163

Preparing an Envelope 163
Printing an Envelope 163
Preparing a Merge Envelope File 163
Printing Merge Envelopes 163
Tutorial 164 • Exercises 170

Checkpoint 3 171

What You Should Know 171
Review Questions 171
Checkpoint Problems 172

Comprehensive Exercise 175

Index 179

Editor's Foreword

This book is one of many in the Boyd & Fraser *Software Training and Reference (STAR) Series*. The manuals in this Series are intended to provide an exceptionally innovative approach to learning popular application software programs, while at the same time providing a source for future reference—so that skills learned can be applied to constantly changing activities.

The overall development of the STAR Series is based upon the following principles:

- In order for any application software manual to be effective it must be organized with the outlook or orientation of a novice user in mind. A novice intuitively approaches a program from the perspective of what he or she would like "to do" or accomplish, rather than from the command perspective of experienced users. *It is for this reason that the STAR Series utilizes a user-oriented topical sequence.*
- There are common concepts underlying the various application software programs within the same general category (i. e., word processing, spreadsheet, database). If users are able to understand these common concepts, they will more likely take greater advantage of the associated program features. In addition, they will have less difficulty implementing the concepts within some different future program environment. While the "how to" of a particular program feature may change or evolve, the "why" and "when" are less likely to do so. That is, while particular application software skills are often not transferrable between programs, the underlying concepts are. *It is for this reason that each topical presentation within the STAR Series begins with a conceptual discussion.*
- There is no substitute for "learning-by-doing". Complete understanding of the concepts-skill linkage can only really be achieved through hands-on activity. *It is for this reason that each STAR Series topic presentation centers around a hands-on tutorial application, highlighting the skill(s) necessary to implement the program feature.*
- Completion of a particular example alone, however, is insufficient for understanding the various nuances of a skill. *Hence relatively extensive exercises and problems, as well as reference material applicable to generalized situations, is provided within each STAR Series manual.*
- In most other tutorial based software training manuals, the actual keystroke activities required to accomplish a tutorial are all too often lost in the surrounding explanatory material. Many users of these manuals become confused and frustrated. *It is for this reason that the STAR Series provides clear, easily distinguishable tutorial steps and directions.*

Each and every manual within the STAR Series is organized in the same consistent format. The selection of end-user-oriented topics focuses on those most fundamental to effective utilization of the program. In addition, each manual within the same general application software category is organized as similarly as possible, while still allowing for individual program variations.

Each topic begins with a conceptual discussion of the selected program features. In this **concepts section** the feature is defined, and the usefulness and applicability of the feature is presented. The conceptual discussion of the topic is followed by a complete keystroke-by-keystroke **tutorial section**. Each action step is easily identified and numerous screen images provide both useful "status checks" and reassuring positive reinforcement.

Following the tutorial section of the topic presentation is the **procedure summary section**. Procedure summaries provide not only useful review of the required implementation procedures or skills, but also serve as a general keystroke reference for applying those skills to future activities.

Throughout the topic presentation are numerous **tips** that include short items of interest, alternative methods for feature implementation, reference to associated topics, and advice on how to avoid common mistakes or overcome common difficulties. Concluding each topic is an **exercise section** for further hands-on skill development.

Each STAR Series manual is divided into three or more parts, each of which concludes with a **checkpoint**. The checkpoints contain numerous "What You Should Know" items designed to emphasize what can be accomplished within the particular program environment. The checkpoints also contain review questions and problems of intermediate difficulty, focusing on material covered up to that checkpoint. Each manual concludes with a **comprehensive problem** that integrates many of the program features within a single application.

DOS Coverage

In order to keep the overall length (and price) of each STAR Series manual down to a reasonable level, and to avoid the possibly unnecessary repetition of fundamental DOS concepts and skills, it was decided to provide DOS coverage separately through a single stand-alone book. Such DOS operating system coverage may be obtained through *DOS Essentials*, by Rod B. Southworth, an inexpensive sixty-four page booklet also published by Boyd & Fraser.

Instructor's Materials

A comprehensive Instructor's Manual is available for use in conjunction with each STAR Series offering. The Instructor's Manual contains topic overviews, key terms, lecture notes, software suggestions, solutions to all exercises and problems, answers to checkpoint review questions, additional comprehensive exercises and solutions, and over 250 test questions. Also available is an Instructor's Resource Disk containing tutorial, exercise, and problem files in various stages of completion.

Series Philosophy — Diversity and Currency

Boyd & Fraser intends to extend the STAR Series to include coverage of all popular application software programs. In addition, we are committed to providing timely coverage of all program updates and revisions. It is hoped that the consistent STAR Series organization and format will provide a flexible approach to either learning multiple application programs or updating to newer program versions. Please contact your local South-Western/Boyd & Fraser Representative for information on current and future STAR Series offerings.

Introduction to Word Processing

Word processing is an accepted part of daily business life. It is a practical and efficient way to create and communicate information. Word processing gives you the power to hold and distribute information quickly, accurately, and inexpensively.

A word processor used to be a separate, somewhat expensive machine, used by people with special training. The personal computer and software now give anyone with basic keyboarding skill the ability to use word processing after learning a few basic procedures.

Word processing software like WordPerfect runs on an IBM personal computer or a compatible. A document is typed using the computer keyboard much like a typewriter. Typographical errors are easily corrected. You can see your work before you print so you can print error-free documents. You no longer need to use correction fluid or print several times to get it right.

Besides correcting errors, the word processor helps you find errors with spell-checking features. A Spell feature flags misspelled words, offers alternatives, highlights incorrect capitalization, finds spacing errors, locates double-word errors, and may even highlight unusual punctuation patterns. A Thesaurus feature helps you find different words that mean the same thing. You can buy additional utility software that can check your grammar, too.

The editing features allow you to change your mind about the appearance or organization of any document. You can move text to a different location, copy parts of a document into another document, or change the appearance of the printed copy to highlight important points. You can create documents that look like professionally typeset pages rather than typewriter pages.

You can save your work electronically so that you can use reports, letters, or forms repeatedly without retyping. You can type your resume once with your basic data. Then, as you gain new skills or experience, you only need to get the resume and make the changes. If you want to address a proposal to several different people about some project, you can type the proposal once, and then use the Search and Replace feature to personalize the proposal for each recipient.

Reports, letters, memos, resumes, and forms are all easy to do. When you type a multipage report, you can quickly add page numbering and footnotes. If you decide to rearrange the body of the report, the footnotes are automatically renumbered, and so are the pages. You can use table or line draw features to create forms like an invoice.

Most word processing software can import graphic files so that you can insert a picture into a report. You can place charts from a spreadsheet program like Lotus 1-2-3 anywhere in a document. You can use data from a program like dBASE to prepare form letters.

As soon as you become comfortable using a word processing software program, you are likely to find many business and personal uses. Your dependence on pen and paper may be replaced by reliance on the computer.

Getting Started

CONCEPTS

To use WordPerfect 5.1, you first need to load the computer's operating system. After the operating system is started, load WordPerfect from the hard disk. When you are finished working, you must follow the proper steps to exit WordPerfect.

Starting WordPerfect 5.1

7

The method for starting WordPerfect depends on your computer and how it has been set up. Check with your instructor or support person for the proper steps.

You may need to change to the WordPerfect directory. When you are in the same directory as WordPerfect, type the command that loads WordPerfect, usually "WP." On some systems, WordPerfect can be loaded by making a selection from a menu. A **menu** is a list of options from which you make your choice.

The Document Edit Screen

After WordPerfect is loaded the copyright screen is followed by the document Edit screen (see Figure 1.1). The **status line** shows the page, line, and position of the cursor. The **cursor** is a blinking light that marks where text is entered into a document.

Figure 1.1
WordPerfect Screen

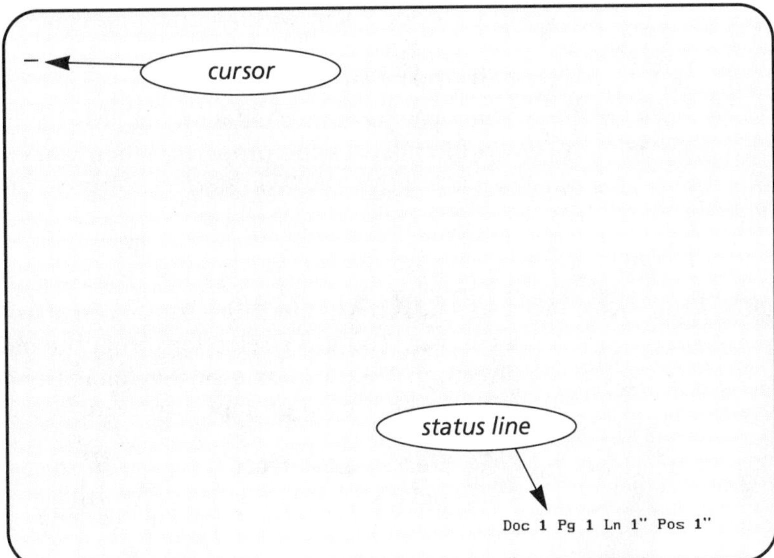

You can also use a mouse to reposition the cursor, make selections from menus, or highlight text on the screen. There may also be a separate mouse pointer in addition to the cursor. The **mouse pointer** is a rectangular block of light.

> **TIP** Whether you use keyboard or menu commands, check the screen for prompts. A prompt is a question or message on the screen that requires a response from you. It helps you determine what to do next. You type or select a response to a prompt.

Using Menus (7)

WordPerfect 5.1 has menus that list major commands. You do not need to remember how to do everything. Just look for it in the menus.

When a menu is displayed, select the command using the keyboard or the mouse. As you make selections, the command is carried out. Often, when you select a command from an initial menu, a related menu appears with another set of options.

Using Keyboard Commands

You can execute WordPerfect commands from the keyboard using the function keys. These function keys are used alone or in combination with the ALTERNATE, CONTROL, or SHIFT key. You can use a WordPerfect keyboard template to check what each function key does. ◄

Checking the Current Directory (7)

You should know which is the current directory. It is where your work will be saved unless you indicate otherwise. If you want to save your work to a floppy disk, the current directory should be set to A:.

Using Help (8)

WordPerfect 5.1 has a context-sensitive Help facility. When you cannot remember how to do something, press F3 (Help) to see an explanation screen. **Context-sensitive** means that WordPerfect displays a Help screen related to what you are doing. If you start Help while trying to save a file, you see a Help screen related to saving files. If you start Help at a blank screen, you see a main Help screen with directions for how to use Help. Help screens are inactive; you can access them, read them, and then return to your document without affecting your work.

Exiting WordPerfect (8)

When you have finished working, it is important that you end your WordPerfect session properly. When you exit, make sure that your work is saved and that the WordPerfect software files are closed.

TUTORIAL

In this tutorial, you start WordPerfect and display the menu bar. You make selections from the menu bar and check the current directory. Then you exit the program. The computer should be turned on with the command prompt displayed.

1 Start WordPerfect.
Make sure you are in the WordPerfect directory.

Type	WP
Press	↵ENTER

The status line is in the lower right corner. The cursor is in the upper left corner.

2 Display and remove the menu bar.

Press	ALT - =	Displays menu bar.
Press	ESC	Removes menu bar.

You can display the menu bar by clicking once on the right mouse button. Click again on the right button to remove the menu.

> **TIP** To make selections with the mouse, position the mouse pointer on the name of the option and click once on the left button. Use the right mouse button to display or remove the menu.

3 Select items from the menu.

Press	ALT - =	Displays menu bar.
Press	H	Displays Help menu.

Menu items are selected by typing the highlighted or underlined letter in the name of the option. You can also make selections using the Arrow keys to highlight your choice; then press the ENTER key. ◀

Press	ESC	Removes Help menu.
Press	F	Displays File menu.
Press	↓ eight times	Related menus appear.

If a menu option has a submenu, it appears with a triangle (▶). Some menu items list equivalent keyboard commands, but you cannot use keyboard commands from within the menu.

Press	ESC twice	Removes menus.

4 Check the current directory.

Place a formatted disk in drive A.

> **TIP** You can execute the List Files command from the keyboard with the F5 key.

Press	ALT - =	Displays menu bar.
Press	↵ENTER	Selects File menu.

Make your selections using the keyboard or the mouse. ◀

Select	"List Files"	Displays current directory name.
Press	=	Displays "New directory" prompt.

The prompt is "New directory" with the name of the current directory.

Type	a:	Stores your work on drive A:.
Press	↵ ENTER	Displays "A:*.* "
Press	ESC	Removes directory prompt.
Press	F5	Displays current directory name.
Press	ESC	Removes directory prompt.

When you change the current directory, the setting remains in effect until you change it again. You should only need to do this once per work session. If you use a mouse, you can click on the right mouse button instead of pressing Enter.

5 **Use Help.** Make your menu selections as explained in step 4 of this tutorial.

Press	ALT-=	Displays menu bar.
Select	"Help"	Displays Help menu.
Select	"Help"	Displays main Help screen.

The main Help screen displays a license number and a version date.

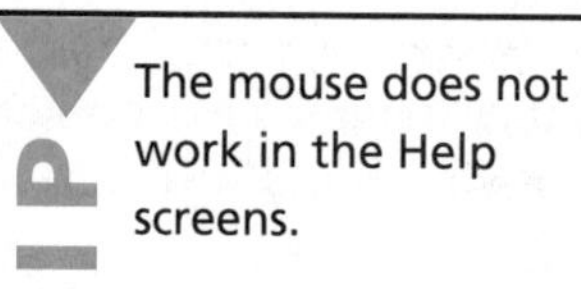
TIP
The mouse does not work in the Help screens.

Press	L	Displays features beginning with "L."
Press	L	Displays additional features.

To look up an option in a Help screen, type the keystrokes shown in the third column. ◀

Press	F5	Displays List Files screen.
Press	1 or R	Displays Retrieve screen.
Press	DELETE	Displays Delete screen.
Press	↵ ENTER	Removes Help screen.

You can execute the Help command from the keyboard with the F3 key.

> **TIP** You can also position the mouse pointer on your choice and click once on the left button.

> **TIP** You can execute the Exit command from the keyboard with the F7 key.

6 Exit WordPerfect.

Press	ALT-=	Displays menu bar.
Select	"File"	Displays File menu.
Select	"Exit"	Displays "Save document?"

Answer the prompt by typing the highlighted letter. To leave the program without saving the document, type "n." ◀

Select	"No"	Displays "Exit WP?"
Select	"Yes"	Exits WordPerfect.

The screen returns to the command prompt or the startup menu. ◀

PROCEDURE SUMMARY

STARTING WORDPERFECT 5.1

Change to the WordPerfect program directory.	
At the command prompt, type the command to start WordPerfect.	WP
Press Enter.	↵ ENTER

USING MENUS

Use the keyboard or the right mouse button to display the menu bar.	ALT-=
Use the keyboard or the left mouse button to make a menu selection.	(your input)

CHECKING THE CURRENT DIRECTORY

Activate the menu bar.	ALT-=
Select "File."	F
Select "List Files."	F
To accept the current directory	ESC
or	
To change the current directory	=
Type the new directory.	(your input)

Accept the new directory.	↵ ENTER
Return to the document.	ESC

USING HELP

Activate the menu bar.	ALT - =
Select "Help."	H
Select "Help."	H
Display a list of topics by typing the first letter in the command.	(your input)
Display a Help screen by typing the keystrokes in the third column.	(your input)
Remove the Help screen.	↵ ENTER

EXITING WORDPERFECT

Activate the menu bar.	ALT - =
Select "File."	F
Select "Exit."	X
Respond to the "Save document?" prompt.	(your input)
Respond to the "Exit WP?" prompt.	Y

EXERCISE

1A Complete the following tasks:

1. Start WordPerfect.
2. Check the current directory for your files.
3. Insert a formatted disk in drive A. Change the current directory to A:.
4. Display the main menu bar. Remove the menu.
5. Display the main Help screen.
6. Display the help list for commands that begin with "E."
7. Read the Help screen about the Exit command.
8. Exit the Help screen, then exit WordPerfect.

Creating and Saving a New Document

CONCEPTS

A document is typed on the screen. You can move the cursor anywhere within the text once it is on the screen to make corrections. A document must be saved on disk if you want to use it again. When you are ready to start work on a new document, you need to clear the screen.

Typing Text

13

When you type a character into a document, the character appears at the cursor location. The cursor then moves one space to the right.

WordPerfect has a wordwrap feature that ends lines at the right margin. You do not press ENTER except at the ends of short lines or at the end of a paragraph. If you were to press ENTER at the end of each line, WordPerfect would not be able to rewrite the screen when you make changes.

WordPerfect operates in Insert mode by default. Whatever you type is added to what is on the screen. Some word processing software is in Strikeover mode, and what you type replaces what it is on the screen. WordPerfect has "Typeover" ability.

The BACKSPACE key erases the character to the left of the cursor, so that you can backspace to correct errors as you type. The TAB key indents a paragraph or aligns columns of text. WordPerfect has default tab settings so that you can use the TAB key without setting tabs.

The CAPS LOCK key affects alphabetic characters, not number or symbol keys. If CAPS LOCK is on and you type "4" from the top row of keys, a "4" appears, not a "$." With CAPS LOCK on, you need to press a SHIFT key to type a dollar sign.

> **TIP** To use the keys in the ten-key pad for cursor movement, the NumLock key must be off. The word "Pos" in the status line blinks when NumLock is on.

Moving the Cursor

13

The cursor can be moved only within text on the screen. If no text is on the screen, the cursor has nowhere to move. The cursor needs to be moved for changes such as inserting or deleting letters. Cursor position is important when you start some commands, too.

Basic cursor movement is with the Arrow keys. You can position the cursor at any location by moving the mouse pointer to the character and clicking on the left button. WordPerfect also has the following shortcuts for moving the cursor (Table 2.1).

Table 2.1
WordPerfect Cursor Commands

Pressing	Moves the cursor
↓	Down one line
↑	Up one line
→	Right one character
←	Left one character
CTRL-↓	Down to next paragraph (enhanced keyboard)
CTRL-←	Left to previous word
CTRL-→	Right to next word
CTRL-↑	Up to previous paragraph (enhanced keyboard)
HOME, ←	Left to edge of screen
HOME, →	Right to edge of screen
END	Right to end of line
PAGE UP	Top of page
PAGE DOWN	Bottom of page

TIP: Use lowercase letters to type a filename. Do not use spaces, commas, or back-slashes in a filename. You may use alphabetic characters, numbers, and most symbols.

Saving the Document

13

After you type a document, your work is on the screen and in RAM. If electrical power is lost or the computer is turned off, the computer's memory is gone and so is your work. A document must be saved to disk if you want to refer to it again. Saving your work periodically is a good habit.

To save a document, you must first determine a name for the file. A filename can be eight or fewer characters. You can use an extension to name documents if you wish. WordPerfect does not automatically assign extensions for word processing documents. ◀

A document is saved to the current directory. If you want to save a document to a different location, type the full pathname such as B:TOPIC2 or C:\FILES\TOPIC2.

Clearing the Screen

13

After a document is saved and printed, you need to clear the screen to start work on something else. You might also want to clear the screen if your first attempt is wrong, and you just want to start over.

When you erase a document from the screen, it is removed from the computer's memory. It is not erased from disk.

4 3699

TUTORIAL

In this tutorial, you type a short document, move the cursor, save your work, and clear the screen. WordPerfect should be started. If you need to check and/or change the current directory, do so (see Topic 1). Insert your document disk in drive A: to save your work.

1 Type the text.

Press	TAB	Indents paragraph.

Type the following paragraph. Do not press Enter until you reach the end of the paragraph. Press Backspace to correct errors as you type.

```
   WordPerfect is a powerful but practical word pro-
cessing program. It can be used for everyday work or
for corporate communications. It has keyboard
commands as well as pull-down menus. There are many
cursor movement commands including several shortcuts.
The mouse can also be used to move the cursor.
```

Press	↵ ENTER	Ends paragraph.

2 Move the cursor.

Press	PAGE UP	Moves cursor to top of page.
Press	PAGE DOWN	Moves cursor to bottom of page.
Press	PAGE UP	Moves cursor to top of page.
Press	CTRL-→ three times	Moves cursor one word to right each time.
Press	CTRL-← twice	Moves cursor one word to left each time.
Press	PAGE UP	Moves cursor to top of page.
Press	HOME, END	Moves cursor to end of line.
Press	HOME, ←	Moves cursor to beginning of line.
Press	HOME, →	Moves cursor to end of line.

This command is similar to HOME, END.

Press	HOME, ←	Moves cursor to beginning of line.
Press	END	Moves cursor to end of line.
Press	PAGE UP	Moves cursor to top of page.
Press	→, ←	Moves cursor left or right one character.
Press	↓, ↑	Moves cursor up or down one line.

3 **Save the document.** The cursor can be located anywhere in the document when you start the Save command.

Press	ALT-=	Displays the menu bar.
Press	F	Displays File menu.
Select	"Save"	Displays "Document to be saved."
Type	topic2	Enters filename.
Press	↵ENTER	Saves document.

> TIP: You can execute the Save command from the keyboard with the F10 key.

After a document is saved, the filename appears in the lower left corner. ◀

4 **Clear the screen.**

Press	ALT-=	Displays menu bar.
Select	"File"	Displays File menu.
Select	"Exit"	Displays "Save document?"
Select	"No"	Displays "Exit WP?"

The document is already saved. The command to clear the screen starts like the Exit command. When your work has not been revised since the last time you saved it, a message appears in the lower right corner, "Text was not modified."

> TIP: You can execute the Exit command from the keyboard with the F7 key.

Select	"No"	Clears screen.

The document is cleared from the screen and memory, but it is still on disk. ◀

PROCEDURE SUMMARY

TYPING TEXT

Type characters.	(your input)
To end a paragraph or a short line	↵ ENTER
To erase errors to the left of the cursor	← BACKSPACE

MOVING THE CURSOR

See Table 2.1 on page 10.

SAVING THE DOCUMENT

Activate the menu bar.	ALT - =
Select "File."	F
Select "Save."	S
Type the filename.	(your input)
Press Enter.	↵ ENTER

CLEARING THE SCREEN

Activate the menu bar.	ALT - =
Select "File."	F
Select "Exit."	X
Respond to "Save document?" prompt.	(your input)
Respond to "Exit WP?" prompt.	N

EXERCISES

2A Complete the following tasks:

1. Start WordPerfect or clear the screen if it is already started.
2. Check the current directory and change it if necessary.
3. Type the following paragraphs. Press the TAB key to indent the first line of each paragraph. Press ENTER twice at the end of each paragraph for a double space. Press BACKSPACE to correct errors.

```
   I have learned several things about WordPerfect in
these two first topics. The initial step is to start the
software using the steps that are appropriate for my lab. I
should check the current directory unless I know that the
default is set where I want it to be set.
   The WordPerfect screen is a blank screen with the
cursor marking where the text will appear. The status line
displays the document, the page, the line, and the position.
   Text is typed like it would be on a typewriter except
that there is no need to press ENTER at the ends of most
lines. I press ENTER to end a paragraph or a short line.
The next exercise uses short lines.
   Clearing the screen and exiting WordPerfect are the
same commands. To clear the screen, though, I respond No to
the prompt about exiting WordPerfect.
```

4. Save your work as EXER2A.
5. Clear the screen.
6. Exit WordPerfect or complete the next exercise.

Don't turn in

2B Complete the following tasks:

1. Start WordPerfect or clear the screen if necessary. Check the current directory and change it if necessary.
2. Type the following list of topics. Press ENTER twice after the first line for a double space. Then press ENTER once at the end of each line since they are short lines. Do not press TAB to indent the lines.

```
WordPerfect 5.1
Start the program
Type the text
Move the cursor
Save the document
Clear the screen
Exit the program
```

3. Save your work as EXER2B.
4. Clear the screen.
5. Exit WordPerfect or go on to the next topic.

Revising and Resaving a Document

CONCEPTS If a document has been saved on disk, it can be retrieved or loaded into the computer's memory. Retrieving a file makes it ready and accessible for additional work. If you make changes to your work, you should then resave the document so that the changes are written to disk.

> **TIP** If you make an error typing the filename, you will see the message "ERROR: File not found." Press DELETE or BACKSPACE to erase the incorrect filename and type the correct filename.

Retrieving a File (21)

When you retrieve a document, the original file stays on the disk. A copy of the file is placed in RAM; this is the copy on which you work.

To retrieve a file, you need to know its filename. You can type the filename at the appropriate prompt, but you must know the precise spelling. If you type even one letter incorrectly in the filename, WordPerfect will not be able to find the file.

Listing Files (22)

When you cannot remember the name of a file or you spelled it wrong when you saved it, you can list your files to the screen. You might also need to list your files to retrieve a document that someone else created and that has a filename you do not know.

When you give the command to list the files, WordPerfect displays all the files in the current directory. You can use DOS filters to adjust what is displayed, and you can display lists from other disks or directories.

> **TIP** WordPerfect is in Insert mode by default. The Typeover mode is activated when you press the INSERT key. You can return to Insert mode by pressing the INSERT key again.

Inserting Text (22)

Inserting allows you to correct errors or add information. You can insert text anywhere in a document on the screen. You can also insert missing tabs or returns between paragraphs.

To add text to the end of a file, position the cursor on a new line following the existing text. Then type the new information. To insert text within an existing line, position the cursor at the location for the inserted letter or word. Since WordPerfect is in Insert mode, the existing text is moved to the right as you type new text. The ends of the lines are readjusted by wordwrap.

Deleting Text (22)

You can delete text and page formatting codes such as tabs or returns. If you had originally indented the paragraphs of a report and later changed your mind, you can retrieve the file and delete the tabs.

The Delete command is executed by pressing the DELETE key while the cursor is positioned beneath the character to be deleted. When you press the DELETE key, one character is erased and the line endings are adjusted. To delete three characters, press DELETE three times. WordPerfect has commands to delete groups of characters or blocks of text, too. For example, there are commands to delete a word, a line, or a paragraph.

Undeleting Text (22)

Sometimes you might delete a word or two and then realize that you should not have done so. WordPerfect allows you to "undelete" or undo a deletion. You can undelete text because WordPerfect stores what you have deleted in a temporary pocket of memory known as a **buffer**. As long as the text is in that buffer, you can undelete it. For most word processing software, the undelete feature works only for the most recently deleted text or the last few deletions. WordPerfect remembers your three most recent deletions.

Resaving a File (23)

If you retrieve a file and make changes, those edits are on the screen and in RAM. To permanently save your work, you must save your work to disk whether it is an original document or a revision of an existing document.

When you resave a file, you can use the same filename and overwrite the original file. You can also resave the file using a different filename. Then you have two copies of the file—the original and the revision.

Resaving your work ensures that your disk has the latest version of a document. If you are making revisions to a long report, resave it often for the same reasons you should periodically save any work. All of your work is gone if you have forgotten to save and the power is interrupted, or if you leave WordPerfect without first saving your document.

TUTORIAL

In this tutorial, you retrieve the TOPIC2 file and make changes by inserting and deleting text. You resave your work with the same filename and then with a different filename. WordPerfect should be started. If you need to check and/or change the current directory, do so (see Topic 1). Insert your document disk in drive A: to save your work.

1 Retrieve a file and clear the screen.

Press	ALT-=	Displays menu bar.
Select	"File"	Displays File menu.

Select	"Retrieve"	Displays "Document to be retrieved."
Type	topic2	Enters filename.
Press	↵ ENTER	Retrieves TOPIC2.

You can execute the Retrieve command from the keyboard with the Shift-F10 key.

Press	ALT - =	Displays menu bar.
Select	"File"	Displays File menu.
Select	"Exit"	Displays "Save document?"

When no changes are made to a file, it is not necessary to save it again. WordPerfect displays a message, "Text was not modified," in the lower right corner.

Select	"No"	Displays "Exit WP?"
Select	"No"	Clears screen.

You can execute the Exit command from the keyboard with the F7 key.

2 Retrieve a file using List Files.

Press	ALT - =	Displays menu bar.
Select	"File"	Displays File menu.
Select	"List Files"	Displays current directory name.
Press	↵ ENTER	Displays list of files.

WordPerfect alphabetizes the list of filenames in the current directory from left to right, top to bottom (see Figure 3.1). The menu options are listed at the bottom of the screen.

Figure 3.1
List Files Screen with TOPIC2, EXER2A, and EXER2B

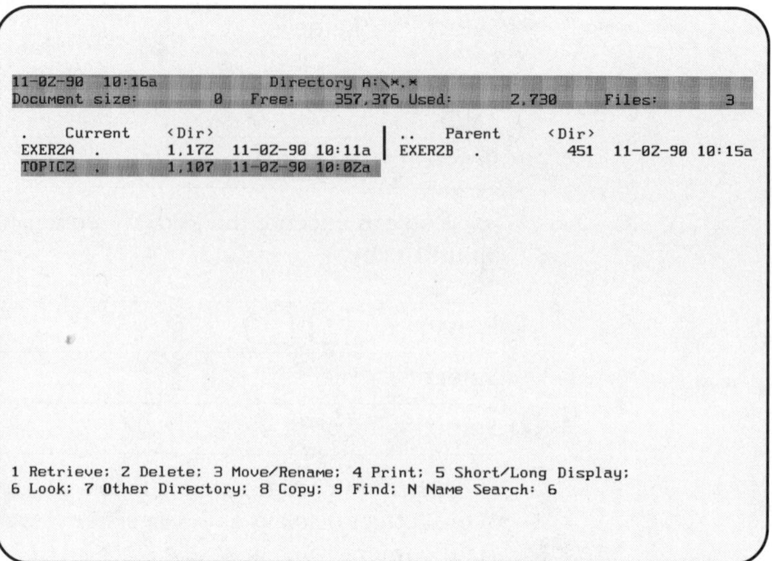

TIP You can remove a files list by pressing the SPACEBAR or a 0 (zero).

Press	↓	Highlights EXER2A filename.
Press	↓	Highlights TOPIC2 filename.

If your list does not match the one in Figure 3.1, use the arrow keys to highlight the TOPIC2 filename. ◀

Select	"Retrieve"	Retrieves TOPIC2.

You can execute the List command from the keyboard with the F5 key.

3 **Insert text.** Watch the screen to determine how many times you need to press the directional arrows or Control-Right Arrow to move the cursor to the "k" in "keyboard."

Press	↓ twice	Moves cursor down two lines.
Press	CTRL-→ three times	Moves cursor to "k" in "keyboard."
Type	quick	Inserts "quick."
Press	SPACEBAR	Inserts space after "quick."
Press	CTRL-→ five times	Moves cursor to "p" in "pull-down."
Type	easy	Inserts "easy."
Press	SPACEBAR	Inserts space after "easy."

Watch the screen to determine how many times you need to press the directional arrows or Control-Right Arrow to move the cursor to the period after "shortcuts."

Press	↓, CTRL-→, →	Moves cursor to the period after "shortcuts."
Press	SPACEBAR	Inserts a space.
Type	for your convenience	Inserts phrase.
Press	↑, CTRL-←	Moves cursor to "I" in "It."

Use cursor movement commands to position the cursor beneath the "I" in "It" in the third sentence if it is not there now.

Press	↵ENTER twice, TAB	Creates new paragraph.

4 **Delete and undelete text.** Watch the screen to determine how many times you need to press the directional arrows or Control-Right Arrow to position the cursor beneath the "a" in "also" in the last sentence.

Press	↓, CTRL-→	Moves cursor to "a" in "also."
Press	DELETE five times	Deletes "also" and the space.
Press	↑, CTRL-←	Moves cursor anywhere in "movement."
Press	CTRL-←BACKSPACE	Deletes "movement."
Press	PAGE UP	Moves cursor to top of page.
Press	CTRL-END	Deletes line.
Press	ALT-=	Displays menu bar.
Select	"Edit"	Displays Edit menu.
Select	"Undelete"	Displays last deletion.

The most recent deletion is displayed at the current cursor position.

Select	"Restore"	Undeletes text.

Watch the screen to determine how many times you need to press the directional arrows or Control-Left Arrow to position the cursor beneath the "b" in "be" in the last sentence.

Press	↓, CTRL-←	Moves cursor to "b" in "be."
Press	ALT-=	Displays menu bar.

Select	"Edit"	Displays Edit menu.
Select	"Undelete"	Displays most recent deletion.
Select	"Previous Deletion"	Displays next most recent deletion.
Select	"Previous Deletion"	Displays "also."

WordPerfect stores your last three deletions in memory. When you delete a fourth time, the first deletion is replaced.

Select	"Restore"	Undeletes "also."
Press	PAGE UP	Moves cursor to top of page.
Press	DELETE	Deletes tab.
Press	ALT-=	Displays menu bar.
Select	"Edit"	Displays Edit menu.
Select	"Undelete"	Displays tab.
Select	"Restore"	Undeletes tab.

TIP: You can use UNDELETE to move text. Delete the text, move the cursor to the new location, and restore the text in the new location.

You can execute the Undelete command from the keyboard with the F1 key.

5 Use Typeover. Watch the screen to determine how many times you need to press the directional arrows, Control-Left Arrow, or Control-Right Arrow to position the cursor beneath the "p" in "program" in the first sentence.

Press	↓, CTRL-←	Moves cursor to "p" in "program."
Press	INSERT	Displays "Typeover."
Type	package	Types over word.
Press	CTRL-→	Moves cursor to "c" in "corporate."
Type	business	Types over word.

There is an extra "e."

Press	DELETE	Deletes "e."
Press	INSERT	Returns WordPerfect to Insert mode.

6 **Resave a file with the same name.**

Press	ALT - =	Displays menu bar.
Select	"File"	Displays File menu.
Select	"Save"	Displays "Document to be saved: A:\TOPIC2."
Press	↵ ENTER	Accepts same filename.
Select	"Yes"	Replaces file on disk.

You can execute the Save command from the keyboard with the F10 key.

7 **Resave a file with a different name.**
TOPIC2 is still on the screen.

Press	ALT - =	Displays menu bar.
Select	"File"	Displays File menu.
Select	"Save"	Displays "Document to be saved: A:TOPIC2."
Press	CTRL - END	Deletes filename.
Type	topic3	Enters new filename.
Press	↵ ENTER	Saves TOPIC3 on disk.
Press	ALT - =	Displays menu bar.
Select	"File"	Displays File menu.
Select	"Exit"	Displays "Save document?"
Select	"No"	Displays "Exit WP?"
Select	"No"	Clears screen.

You can execute the Exit command from the keyboard with the F7 key.

PROCEDURE SUMMARY

RETRIEVING A FILE

Start with a clean screen.	
Activate the menu bar.	ALT - =
Select "File."	F
Select "Retrieve."	R

Type the filename with a path if the file is not in the current directory.	(your input)
Retrieve the file.	↵ ENTER

LISTING FILES

Start with a clean screen.	
Activate the menu bar.	ALT-=
Select "File."	F
Select "List Files."	F
Accept the current directory.	↵ ENTER
Highlight the filename in the list.	(your input)
Retrieve the file.	1 or R

INSERTING TEXT

WordPerfect defaults to Insert mode. If "Typeover" appears in the lower left corner, press Insert to return to Insert mode.	
Position cursor where new text is to appear and begin typing.	(your input)

DELETING TEXT

Position cursor beneath character.	DELETE
Position cursor anywhere in a word.	CTRL-←BACKSPACE
Position cursor on first character of line.	CTRL-END
Position cursor on first character of page.	CTRL-PAGE DOWN
Respond to "Delete remainder of page" prompt.	Y

UNDELETING TEXT

Activate the menu bar.	ALT-=
Select "Edit."	E
Select "Undelete."	U
Select the correct deletion.	(your input)
Restore the text at the cursor position.	1 or R

RESAVING A FILE

To resave a document using the same filename:

Activate the menu bar.	ALT-=
Select "File."	F
Select "Save."	S
Accept the current filename.	↵ ENTER
Replace the existing document.	Y

To resave a document using a different filename:

Activate the menu bar.	ALT-=
Select "File."	F
Select "Save."	S
Delete the current filename.	CTRL-END
Type new filename and path if different from current directory.	(your input)
Save the file.	↵ ENTER

EXERCISES

3A **Complete the following tasks:**

Don't turn in

1. Retrieve EXER2A.
2. In the first paragraph, delete "these two" and insert "the" and "three" so that the sentence reads "in the first three topics."
3. Press PAGE DOWN to position the cursor at the end of the text. Press ENTER one time if the cursor is not at Pos 1.

4. Add the following paragraphs.

```
     After a file has been saved to disk, it can be
retrieved from the disk. Retrieving a file places a copy of
the document into the machine's memory. That file can then
be resaved using the same name.
   I can insert and delete text to correct errors or
make other necessary revisions. In addition to inserting
letters or words, I can insert tabs and returns.
```

5. Use Insert and Delete to correct errors.
6. Resave the document as EXER2A.
7. Clear the screen.
8. Exit WordPerfect or complete the next exercise.

3B Complete the following tasks:

1. Retrieve EXER2B.
2. Position the cursor beneath the "T" in "Type" and insert a return by pressing ENTER.
3. Return the cursor to the blank line and type "Check the current directory."
4. Press PAGE DOWN to position the cursor at the end of the text. Press ENTER one time if the cursor is not at Pos 1.
5. Add the following lines.

```
Retrieve a file
Delete and undelete text
Insert text
Resave a file using the same or a different name
```

6. Use Insert or Delete to correct errors.
7. Save your work as a new file named EXER3B.
8. Clear the screen.
9. Exit WordPerfect or go on to the next topic.

Printing a Document

CONCEPTS With word processing software like WordPerfect, the screen does not always match the printed copy. Mismatches are caused by different letter sizes, underline, italic, page numbers, and header or footers. You may have entered the commands for such features, but you may not see the results until the document is printed.

Previewing a Document

29

Before you send a document to the printer, you can preview it. You can determine if the margins and spacing are correct, if lines are centered, and if tabs are properly positioned. Without a preview, you may not find formatting errors until you see the printed copy.

When you view a document, the screen may show a reduced version of the page. You can get an overall impression of the appearance of your work. In most packages, including WordPerfect 5.1, you cannot make any changes while you are in View mode.

Printing a Page

When a document is on the screen, you give the print command to send the information to the printer. WordPerfect and the printer determine what size type to use and how to handle the paper. With a laser printer, paper is stored in a tray and is automatically fed sheet by sheet. A dot matrix printer with continuous-feed paper handles the paper automatically by pulling up a new sheet when necessary. ◀

> **TIP** The size and style of printed characters is referred to as the font. Laser and dot matrix printers generally have several fonts. One font is the default. This is the printed type size and style for all documents, unless you make a change.

You can print one page at a time, specific pages, or the entire document. You can choose to print more than one copy of a document, too. With WordPerfect, you can print only the odd or even pages of a document.

Printing from the List

Most word processing software prints the document that is on the screen. You can also print a document that is on disk, but not on the screen. With this feature, you can print one document and use the screen to start another file. You do not have to wait until the first document is finished printing.

TIP

A queue is a waiting line of print jobs. Printers have memories and can store multiple documents and print them in turn. When a document is in the queue, the print job can be canceled and removed from the queue.

Canceling a Print Job

29

When a document is sent to the printer, the file is listed as a job in a queue. WordPerfect prepares the job for printing and then releases it to the printer. For a short document, the page is printed quickly. For long documents, WordPerfect prepares the pages and sends them to the printer one page at a time. ◄

For short documents, you will find that the document is printed before you can complete the steps to cancel it. If a long document is printing when you notice an error, you can cancel it so that you do not waste paper printing the rest of it. If you cannot wait for a long document to finish printing, you can cancel it and print it some other time.

TUTORIAL

In this tutorial, you preview and print a document from the screen and from the list of files. You also cancel a print command. WordPerfect should be started. If you need to check and/or change the current directory, do so. Insert your document disk in drive A: to save your work.

1 View a document.

Press	ALT-=	Displays menu bar.
Select	"File," "Retrieve"	Displays Retrieve prompt.
Type	exer2a	Enters filename.
Press	↵ ENTER	Retrieves EXER2A.

You can execute the Retrieve command from the keyboard with the Shift-F10 key.

Press	ALT-=	Displays menu bar.
Select	"File," "Print"	Displays Print menu.

The View Document option is part of the Print menu.

Select	"View Document"	Displays EXER2A as it will print.

You can select from four views of the page (100%, 200%, Full Page, or Facing Pages). WordPerfect displays the last selected size.

Press	SPACEBAR	Removes View screen.
Press	SPACEBAR	Removes Print menu.

You can click on the right mouse button to remove the View Document screen. You can execute the View Document command from the keyboard with the Shift-F7 key.

2 **Print a page.** Make sure the printer is ready. With a single-page document, you can print by Full Document or Page.

Press	ALT - =	Displays menu bar.
Select	"File," "Print"	Displays Print menu.
Select	"Page"	Prints page.

After the page is printed, the Print menu is removed from the screen. You can execute the Print command from the keyboard with the Shift-F7 key.

Press	ALT - =	Displays menu bar.
Select	"File," "Exit"	Displays Save prompt.
Select	"No"	Displays Exit prompt.
Select	"No"	Clears screen.

You can execute the Exit command from the keyboard with the F7 key.

3 **Print from the list.**

Press	ALT - =	Displays menu bar.
Select	"File," "List Files"	Displays directory name.
Press	↵ ENTER	Lists files.

Use the mouse or the arrow keys to select the filename.

Select	EXER2A	Highlights filename.
Select	"Print"	Displays "Page(s): (All)".

You can specify a range of pages such as "2-4," a single page, or all pages.

Press	↵ ENTER	Prints all pages.
Press	SPACEBAR	Removes list.

You can execute the List command from the keyboard with the F5 key.

4 **Cancel a print job.** Take your printer offline or turn it off so that it is not ready.

Press	ALT-=	Displays menu bar.
Select	"File," "Retrieve"	Displays Retrieve prompt.
Type	topic2	Enters filename.
Press	↵ENTER	Retrieves TOPIC2.
Press	ALT-=	Displays menu bar.
Select	"File," "Print"	Displays Print menu.
Select	"Full Document"	Sends document to printer.
Press	ALT-=	Displays menu bar.
Select	"File," "Print"	Displays Print menu.
Select	"Control Printer"	Displays print job status.

The document is in the print queue, but the printer is not ready. The Message and Action lines show possible solutions.

Select	"Cancel Job(s)"	Displays "Cancel which job?"
Press	↵ENTER	Cancels current job.

When the job is canceled, the Control Printer menu shows an empty Job List. Check the screen for an additional message on the Action line. You may need to reset the printer by typing a "g".

Press	↵ENTER twice	Removes Print menus.

Turn the printer on or set it online.

Press	ALT-=	Displays menu bar.
Select	"File," "Exit"	Displays Save prompt.
Select	"No"	Displays Exit prompt.
Select	"No"	Clears screen.

PROCEDURE SUMMARY

PREVIEWING A DOCUMENT

Activate the menu bar.	ALT-=
Select "File."	F
Select "Print."	P
Select "View Document."	V or 6
Resize the view.	1 or 2 or 3 or 4
Return to the document.	SPACEBAR twice

PRINTING A PAGE

Activate the menu bar.	ALT-=
Select "File."	F
Select "Print."	P
Select the amount to be printed.	(your input)

PRINTING FROM THE LIST

Activate the menu bar.	ALT-=
Select "File."	F
Select "List."	F
Accept the current directory.	↵ ENTER
Highlight the filename.	(your input)
Select the option to print.	P or 4
Respond to the pages prompt.	(your input)

CANCELING A PRINT JOB

Activate the menu bar.	ALT-=
Select "File."	F
Select "Print."	P
Select the Printer Control option.	C or 4
Select the Cancel Jobs option.	C or 1
Accept the job number.	↵ ENTER
Check the Action line for messages.	
Return to the document.	↵ ENTER twice

EXERCISES

4A Complete the following tasks:

1. Type the following paragraphs. Press TAB to indent the first line of each paragraph. Press ENTER twice at the end of each paragraph. Correct errors as you type.

    The ability to get along with others is probably one of the greatest assets any student or worker can have. Even if you are highly skilled and talented in a class or job, you may be miserable if you cannot get along with classmates or fellow workers.

    Although society changes rapidly, the old-fashioned art of good manners is still valued. One of the first rules in any group setting is to be courteous to everyone. Never forget to use words such as "please," "thank you," and "excuse me."

    Be a good listener and show concern about others. Most of us have the bad habit of talking but never listening to what others say. It may take an effort on your part to listen more and talk less.

2. Save your work as EXER4A and leave the document on the screen.
3. Print EXER4A while it is on the screen.
4. Exit WordPerfect or complete the next exercise.

4B Complete the following tasks:

1. List the files on your disk. Print EXER4A from the list.
2. As soon as you have given the print command, press the SPACEBAR to return to the document screen. Type your name while EXER4A is printing.
3. Exit WordPerfect or go on to the next topic.

Setting and Changing Margins

> **TIP** Printer fonts are either monospaced or proportional. A monospaced font is measured in cpi, characters per inch. Each character occupies the same amount of space when printed. Popular sizes are 10 and 12 cpi. A proportional font is measured in points. Letters occupy space according to their formation. A "W" requires more space on the line than an "I." Popular proportional sizes are 10, 11, and 12 points.

> **TIP** Most laser printers have an "unprintable" region on the paper, usually about ¼ inch on all edges. You cannot set a margin as small as ⅛ inch because the printer cannot reach that area. WordPerfect automatically adjusts such small margins to the printer minimum setting.

CONCEPTS Margins frame your work with white space. Margins should be balanced so that your work appears well positioned on the page. You can use margins to fit more or less text on a page because you can type more on a page with 0.75-inch side margins than on a page with 1-inch margins.

Setting Left and Right Margins

38

Word processing software has default left and right margin settings based on standard paper sizes. If you want to type a postcard or an envelope, however, you should change the margins to fit the size of the postcard or the envelope. You might also need to change the margins so that text aligns with a letterhead logo.

Margins are set using inches or spaces; WordPerfect uses inches. The default left and right margins are 1 inch. Using spaces to set margins is similar to the way margins are set on a typewriter. 

Setting Top and Bottom Margins

38

Like left and right margins, top and bottom margins frame your work with white space. Top and bottom margins also control the placement of headers, footers, and page numbers. If you want to change the location of any of these options, you need to change the top or bottom margins.

You can use a ruler to determine how much top or bottom margin to set. One-inch top and bottom margins are the default settings. 

Changing Margins

39

Left and right margins can be changed as many times as necessary in a document. You can type the first part of a document with 1-inch margins and the second part with 2-inch margins. You can change margins after a document has been typed if you decide that it might look better with wider or narrower margins.

Top and bottom margins can also be changed, but each page can have only one setting. When you change any margin, that setting becomes effective for the rest of the document or until you make another change.

Deleting a Code

39

WordPerfect displays codes when you give the Reveal Codes command. The screen splits into two windows—one with the regular document and one with the coded document. An **electronic code** is a symbol or a command inserted in the text for formatting or display. A return or a tab is an electronic code. The codes to change the font and the margins are two more examples of electronic codes.

You need to understand codes so that you can delete them, insert them, or change them. If you want to change the margins, you must realize that a code somewhere in the document needs to be adjusted.

Most codes are deleted or inserted with regular Delete and Insert procedures. Once the cursor is positioned, you usually only need to delete or change the code to reformat the document or part of it. ◀

TIP In WordPerfect, codes are deleted by pressing DELETE when the cursor is on the code. If the cursor is one character to the right of the code, delete it by pressing BACKSPACE.

Inserting a Code

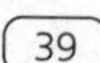

Some word processing software include one main code to specify all margin settings. If you change that code, all margins are adjusted. Other packages, like WordPerfect, allow you to place many margin codes in a document. When you insert new codes, you may need to delete old codes. If you have unnecessary codes in a document, you are more likely to have unexpected formatting.

TUTORIAL

In this tutorial, you insert and delete electronic codes such as tabs, returns, and margins. You type and save a document using different margin settings. WordPerfect should be started. If you need to check and/or change the current directory, do so. Insert your document disk in drive A: to save your work.

1 Reveal the codes.

Press	ALT - =	Displays menu bar.
Select	"File," "Retrieve"	Displays Retrieve prompt.
Type	exer4a	Enters filename.
Press	↵ ENTER	Retrieves EXER4A.

You can execute the Retrieve command from the keyboard with the Shift-F10 key.

Press	ALT - =	Displays menu bar.
Select	"Edit"	Displays Edit menu.
Select	"Reveal Codes"	Displays Codes screen.

The screen splits into two windows with 12 lines of regular text at the top. A reverse-video horizontal bar separates the windows. The lower window shows the same text with electronic codes in square brackets. The triangles in the reverse-video bar are tab settings. The curly braces or square brackets in the reverse-video bar show the left and right margins. You can execute the Reveal Codes command from the keyboard with the F11 key.

Press	END	Moves cursor to end of line.

The cursor moves in both windows. [SRt] is a code for "soft return," a line ending where wordwrap has occurred.

Press	ALT-=	Displays menu bar.
Select	"Search"	Displays Search menu.
Select	"Go To"	Displays "Go to."
Press	↵ ENTER	Moves cursor to [HRt] code.

TIP You can respond to the "Go to" prompt with a page number, a text character, or a code. If you use a page number, press ENTER after typing the number.

[HRt] means "hard return," a line ending where you pressed Enter. You can execute the Go To command from the keyboard with the Control-Home key.

Press	→	Moves cursor to [Tab] code.

Figure 5.1
EXER4A with Codes Revealed

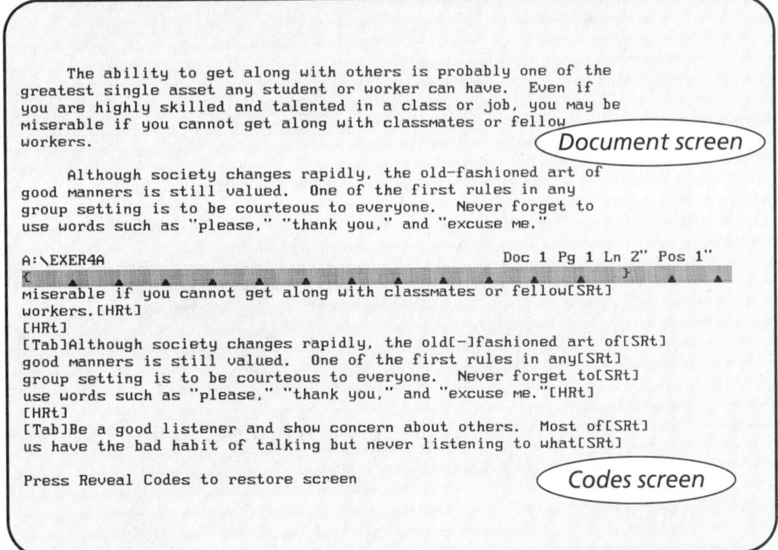

Press	ALT-=	Displays menu bar.
Select	"Edit," "Reveal Codes"	Removes Codes screen.

> **TIP** The Reveal Codes command is faster from the keyboard. If you have a standard keyboard, press ALT-F3 to reveal the codes.

2 Delete a code.

Press	HOME twice, ↑	Moves cursor to top of document.
Press	F11	Displays Codes screen.

The screen splits into two windows. The cursor should be on the [Tab] code in the lower window. ◀

Press	DELETE	Deletes [Tab] code.

The text starts at the left margin.

Press	ALT-=	Displays menu bar.
Select	"Search," "Go To"	Displays "Go to."
Press	TAB	Moves cursor to "A."

The Go To command moves one space to the right of the first occurrence of the character you type. It is now one character to the right of the [Tab] code.

Press	←BACKSPACE	Deletes the [Tab] code.
Press	ALT-=	Displays menu bar.
Select	"Search," "Go To"	Displays "Go to."
Press	TAB	Moves cursor to "B" in "Be."
Press	←BACKSPACE	Deletes [Tab] code.

3 Insert a code.

Press	HOME twice, ↑	Moves cursor to top of document.
Press	TAB	Inserts [Tab] code.

A [Tab] code is inserted in the bottom window. The text is indented in the top window.

Press	ALT-=	Displays menu bar.
Select	"Search," "Go To"	Displays "Go to."
Press	↵ENTER	Moves cursor to [HRt] code.

Press	→	Moves cursor to "A" in "Although."
Press	TAB	Inserts [Tab] code.
Press	ALT-=	Displays menu bar.
Select	"Search," "Go To"	Displays "Go To."
Press	↵ ENTER	Moves cursor to next [HRt].

The Go To command searches forward from the current cursor position. The cursor is now at the end of the second paragraph.

Press	→	Moves cursor to "B" in "Be."
Press	TAB	Inserts [Tab] code.
Press	F11	Removes Codes screen.
Press	ALT-=	Displays menu bar.
Select	"File," "Exit"	Displays Save prompt.
Select	"No"	Displays Exit prompt.
Select	"No"	Clears screen.

4 Set margins.

Press	ALT-=	Displays menu bar.
Select	"Layout"	Displays Layout menu.
Select	"Page"	Displays Page Format menu.
Select	"Margins"	Moves cursor to top margin field.
Type	1.5	Enters new top margin.
Press	↵ ENTER	Moves cursor to bottom margin field.
Press	↵ ENTER	Accepts margins.
Press	↵ ENTER	Displays main Format menu.
Press	↵ ENTER	Displays Edit screen.

TIP The main Format menu appears when you start format commands from the keyboard. When entering measurements, you can type fractions such as 1/2. WordPerfect converts them to decimals.

The status line shows the new top margin as Ln 1.5". You can execute the Top/Bottom Margin command from the keyboard with the Shift-F8 key. ◀

Press	F11	Displays Codes screen.

A [T/B Mar:1.5",1"] code has been placed in your document.

Press	F11	Removes Codes screen.
Press	TAB	Indents paragraph.

Type the following paragraph.

```
   In the battle for effectiveness, legible text is not
enough. Using the correct font will help to win the war for
your reader's attention.
```

Press	↵ENTER twice	Ends paragraph.
Press	ALT-=	Displays menu bar.
Select	"Layout"	Displays Layout menu.
Select	"Line"	Displays Line Format menu.
Select	"Margins"	Moves cursor to left margin field.
Type	1.5	Enters new left margin.
Press	↵ENTER	Moves cursor to right margin field.
Type	1.5	Enters new right margin.
Press	↵ENTER	Accepts new margins.
Press	↵ENTER	Displays main Format menu.
Press	↵ENTER	Returns to document.

The status line shows the new left margin as Pos 1.5". You can execute the Left/Right Margins command from the keyboard with the Shift-F8 key.

Press	F11	Displays Codes screen.

A [L/R Mar:1.5",1.5"] code has been inserted.

Press	F11	Removes Codes screen.
Press	TAB	Indents paragraph.

Type the following paragraph.

```
   A font is a set of characters that have the same size,
weight, and slant. A proportional font gives each letter a
relative amount of horizontal space depending on the size of
the letter. A monospaced font uses the same horizontal
space for each character.
```

Press	↵ENTER twice	Ends the paragraph.
Press	ALT-=	Displays menu bar.

Select	"File," "Save"	Displays Save prompt.
Type	topic5	Enters filename.
Press	↵ ENTER	Saves document.
Press	ALT - =	Displays menu bar.
Select	"File," "Print"	Displays Print menu.
Select	"Page"	Prints page.

5 Change the margins.

Press	F11	Displays Codes screen.

Watch the bottom window to determine how many times you need to press the directional arrows to move the cursor to the [L/R Mar: 1.5",1.5"] code before the second paragraph.

Press	↑, ←	Moves cursor to [L/R Mar: 1.5",1.5"] code.
Press	DELETE	Deletes [L/R Mar] code.

Both paragraphs now use the 1-inch default left margin.

Press	HOME twice, ↑	Moves cursor to top of document.
Press	ALT - =	Displays menu bar.
Select	"Layout," "Line"	Displays Line Format menu.
Select	"Margins"	Moves cursor to left margin field.
Type	1.25	Enters new left margin.
Press	↵ ENTER	Moves cursor to right margin field.
Type	1.25	Enters new right margin.
Press	↵ ENTER	Accepts new margins.
Press	F7	Returns to document.

TIP You can return directly to the screen from a menu by pressing F7 or clicking on the right mouse button.

The status line shows the left margin at Pos 1.25". The Codes screen shows the new [L/R Mar] code. ◄

Press	F11	Removes Codes screen.
Press	ALT - =	Display menu bar.

Select	"File," "Print," "View Document"	Displays View screen.
Press	SPACEBAR twice	Returns to document.
Press	ALT - =	Displays menu bar.
Select	"File," "Save"	Displays "Document to be saved: A:\TOPIC5."
Press	↵ENTER	Displays "Replace A:\TOPIC5?"
Select	"Yes"	Replaces TOPIC5.
Press	ALT - =	Displays menu bar.
Select	"File," "Exit"	Displays Save prompt.
Select	"No"	Displays Exit prompt.
Select	"No"	Clears screen.

PROCEDURE SUMMARY

SETTING LEFT AND RIGHT MARGINS

Activate the menu bar.	ALT - =
Select "Layout."	L
Select "Line."	L
Select "Margins."	M or 7
Enter left margin setting.	(your input)
Accept the new margin.	↵ENTER
Enter right margin setting.	(your input)
Accept the new margin.	↵ENTER
Return to the document.	F7 or ↵ENTER twice

SETTING TOP AND BOTTOM MARGINS

Activate the menu bar.	ALT - =
Select "Layout."	L
Select "Page."	P
Select "Margins."	M or 5
Enter top margin setting.	(your input)

Accept the new margin.	↵ ENTER
Enter bottom margin setting.	(your input)
Accept the new margin.	↵ ENTER
Return to the document.	F7 or ↵ ENTER twice

CHANGING MARGINS

Position cursor at location for change.	
Activate the menu bar.	ALT - =
Select "Layout."	L
Select "Line" or "Page."	L or P
Select "Margins."	M or 7 or 5
Enter left or top margin setting.	(your input)
Accept the new margin.	↵ ENTER
Enter right or bottom margin setting.	(your input)
Accept the new margin.	↵ ENTER
Return to the document.	F7 or ↵ ENTER twice

DELETING A CODE

Display the electronic Codes screen.	F11
Position the cursor to the right of or beneath the code.	←BACKSPACE or DELETE

INSERTING A CODE

Display the electronic Codes screen.	F11
Position the cursor where the new code is to be placed.	(your input)
Insert the codes using regular steps.	(your input)

EXERCISES

5A Complete the following tasks:

1. Type the following letter. Press ENTER where indicated. Correct errors as you type.

Your Street Address
Your City, State ZIP
Today's Date (**press ENTER five times**)

WordPerfect Student
Your School's Name
Your School's City, State ZIP (**press ENTER twice**)

Dear New Student: (**press ENTER twice**)

I hope you will be able to learn WordPerfect soon. It has been an interesting and enlightening experience for me. (**press ENTER twice**)

I just learned about electronic codes which is somewhat unusual to the human mind. We are accustomed to seeing everything concrete and on paper. Computers do not work that way, though, so we had better get used to them. (**press ENTER twice**)

I plan to use WordPerfect to type all my notes as well as my class papers and assignments. All this work should earn me a better grade, too! (**press ENTER twice**)

Sincerely yours, (**press ENTER four times**)

YOUR NAME

2. Save your work as EXER5A and leave the document on the screen.
3. Reveal the codes. Look for [SRt] and [HRt] codes. There are no [Tab] codes in this document. Remove the codes.
4. Print EXER5A.
5. Exit WordPerfect or complete the next exercise.

5B Complete the following tasks:

1. Retrieve EXER5A. Reveal the codes.
2. Position the cursor at the beginning of each text paragraph and insert a [Tab] code to indent the paragraphs. Remove the Codes screen.
3. Print EXER5A.
4. Press PAGE UP to position the cursor at the top of the page. Change the left and right margins to 1.25 inches.
5. Save EXER5A as a new file named EXER5B.
6. Print EXER5B.
7. Exit WordPerfect or go on to the next topic.

Setting and Changing Tabs

CONCEPTS Tabs are used to indent the first line of a paragraph or to align columns of text or numbers. Tabs give a consistent, organized appearance to your work when they are set properly. They provide you with a fast, efficient way to prepare your work.

Setting Tabs

46

WordPerfect has default tabs set at 0.5-inch intervals across the page. This is useful for some work, but it could be cumbersome for other projects. If you need to type a form that has one tab halfway across the page, you certainly do not want to have to press TAB five or six times to reach the halfway point. It is more productive to change the tab settings to have just that one tab.

Some word processing software figures tabs from the edge of the page. If you want a tab to appear at 1.5 inches, you set the tab at 1.5 inches. WordPerfect tabs are set relative to the left margin. With the left margin at 1 inch, you set a tab at 0.5 for text to align 1.5 inches from the edge of the page. ◀

TIP: WordPerfect has both kinds of tabs—absolute and relative. Relative is the default.

Changing Tabs

47

Tabs can be changed as many times as necessary in a document. You can type the first part of a document with tabs set 0.5 and 1 inch from the margin. In another section of the document, you can use one tab at the center of the page. You can change tabs after a document has been typed if you decide that the tabs do not look balanced.

Using Different Tab Types

47

Tabs are used to align text on the left when typing tabular information. If tabular data includes numbers, however, you can set a different kind of tab to align the numbers on the right or on the decimal point. Usually the type of tab alignment is specified when you set the tabs. When you reach that point in the document, just press TAB.

In addition to tabs to align numbers, WordPerfect has tabs that can center text at the tab setting. Another popular type of tab setting is a "dot leader" tab, which inserts leaders when you press TAB.

TUTORIAL

In this tutorial, you type and save a document with tabs. Then you change the tab settings to reposition the data. You also type a document with a decimal tab. WordPerfect should be started. If you need to check and/or change the current directory, do so. Insert your document disk in drive A: to save your work.

1 Set tabs.

Press	ALT - =	Displays menu bar.
Select	"File," "Retrieve"	Displays Retrieve prompt.
Type	topic5	Enters filename.
Press	↵ ENTER	Retrieves TOPIC5.
Press	PAGE DOWN	Moves cursor to bottom of document.
Press	ALT - =	Displays menu bar.
Select	"Layout," "Line"	Displays Line Format menu.
Select	"Tab Set"	Displays tab ruler.

The left margin is 0". An "L" marks each tab setting (see Figure 6.1). Tabs to the right of the margin use positive numbers such as +1". Tabs to the left of the margin use negative numbers such as -0.5".

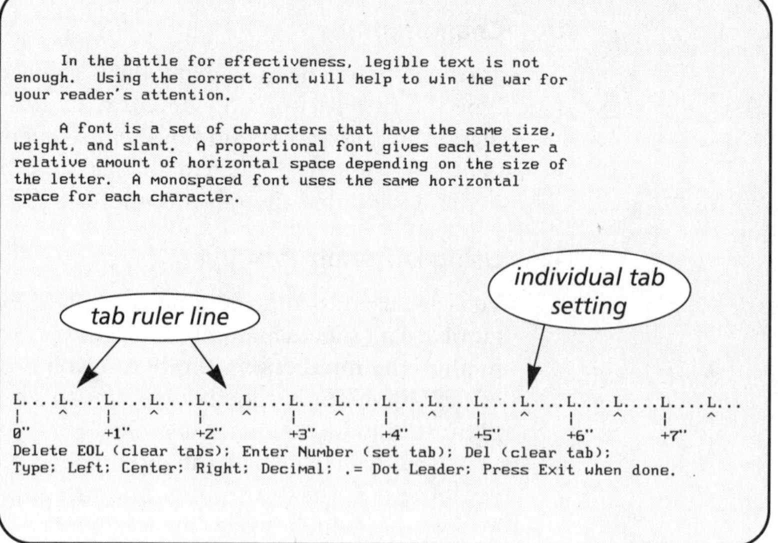

Figure 6.1
TOPIC5 with Tab Ruler Displayed

Press	CTRL - END	Deletes all tabs.

The Delete to End of Line command deletes all tabs from the cursor position forward. You can select Delete EOL with the mouse.

Type	0.75	Enters new tab setting.

The number appears at the lower right corner of the screen. To set a tab less than +1", type the zero before the decimal point.

Press	↵ENTER	Enters "L" at +0.75".
Type	2	Enters new tab setting.
Press	↵ENTER	Enters "L" at +2".
Press	F7	Displays Line Format menu.
Press	F7	Returns to document.

You can execute the Tab Set command from the keyboard with the Shift-F8 key. You can leave the tab ruler line by clicking on the right mouse button.

Press	F11	Displays Codes screen.

A [Tab Set:Rel;-1",-0.5",+0.75",+2"] code has been inserted.

Press	F11	Removes Codes screen.

Type the following paragraph and data. Press Enter twice at the end of the paragraph and at the end of each tabbed line. Press Tab once before the first column and once before the second column.

```
Here is information about font sizes. A larger point size
means a bigger letter. However, a larger pitch means a
smaller letter.

  10 cpi   10 characters per inch, monospaced
  12 cpi   12 characters per inch, monospaced
  16 cpi   16 characters per inch, monospaced
  10 pt    10 points high, proportional
  12 pt    12 points high, proportional
```

Press	↵ENTER twice	Ends file.
Press	ALT - =	Displays menu bar.
Select	"File," "Save"	Displays Save prompt.
Press	END	Moves cursor to end of line.
Press	←BACKSPACE	Deletes 5.

Type	6	Changes filename.
Press	↵ ENTER	Saves TOPIC6.

TOPIC5 is unchanged and still available.

Press	ALT - =	Displays menu bar.
Select	"File," "Print," "Page"	Prints page.

2 Change the tabs.

Press	F11	Displays Codes screen.

Watch the screen to determine how many times to press the directional arrows to move the cursor to the [Tab Set] code as shown in Figure 6.2.

Press	↑, ←	Moves cursor to [Tab Set] code.

Figure 6.2
TOPIC6 Showing Code to Be Deleted

```
     In the battle for effectiveness, legible text is not
enough.  Using the correct font will help to win the war for
your reader's attention.

     A font is a set of characters that have the same size,
weight, and slant.  A proportional font gives each letter a
relative amount of horizontal space depending on the size of
the letter.  A monospaced font uses the same horizontal
space for each character.

Here is information about font sizes.  A larger point size
A:\TOPIC6                                    Doc 1 Pg 1 Ln 2.67" Pos 1.25"
the letter.  A monospaced font uses the same horizontal[SRt]
space for each character.[HRt]
[HRt]
[Tab Set:Rel: -1",-0.5",+0.75",+2"]Here is information about font sizes.  A larg
er point size[SRt]
means a bigger letter.  However, a larger pitch means a[SRt]
smaller letter.[HRt]
[HRt]
[Tab]10 cpi[Tab]10 characters per inch, monospaced[HRt]
[HRt]

Press Reveal Codes to restore screen
```

code to be deleted

Press	DELETE	Deletes [Tab Set] code.

The text now uses the default tab settings.

Press	ALT - =	Displays menu bar.
Select	"Layout," "Line," "Tab Set"	Displays tab ruler.

Press	CTRL-END	Deletes all tabs.
Type	0.5	Enters new tab setting.
Press	↵ ENTER	Enters "L" at +0.5".
Type	2.25	Enters new tab setting.
Press	↵ ENTER	Enters "L" at +2.25".
Press	F7	Displays Line Format menu.
Press	F7	Returns to document.
Press	F11	Displays [Tab Set] code.
Press	F11	Removes Codes screen.
Press	ALT-=	Displays menu bar.
Select	"File," "Exit"	Displays Save prompt.
Select	"Yes"	Displays filename.
Press	↵ ENTER	Displays "Replace A:\TOPIC6?"
Select	"Yes"	Replaces TOPIC6.
Select	"No"	Clears screen.

3 Use a decimal tab.

Press	ALT-=	Displays menu bar.
Select	"Layout," "Line," "Tab Set"	Displays tab ruler.
Press	CTRL-END	Deletes all tabs.
Type	0.75	Enters new tab setting.
Press	↵ ENTER	Enters "L" at +0.75".
Type	4.25	Enters new tab setting.
Press	↵ ENTER	Enters "L" at +4.25".
Type	D	Replaces "L" with "D."

A "D" in the tab ruler sets a decimal tab.

Press	F7	Displays Line Format menu.
Press	F7	Returns to document.
Press	F11	Displays [Tab Set] code.

The [Tab Set] code does not show the type of tab.

Press	F11	Removes Codes screen.
Press	TAB	Moves cursor to Pos 1.75".
Type	Dot Matrix Printer	Aligns text on left.
Press	TAB	Displays "Align char =."

The alignment character for a decimal tab is the decimal point.

Type	$345.50	Aligns number on decimal point.
Press	↵ ENTER	Ends line.
Press	TAB	Moves cursor to Pos 1.75".
Type	Laser Printer	Aligns text on left.
Press	TAB	Displays "Align char =."
Type	$1,250.75	Aligns number on decimal point.
Press	↵ ENTER	Ends line.
Press	F11	Displays [Dec Tab] code.
Press	F11	Removes Codes screen.

Follow the same steps to add two lines to your document. Press Enter after the last line.

```
Dot Matrix Ribbons      $12.25
Laser Printer Toner     $89.00
```

Press	ALT - =	Displays menu bar.
Select	"File," "Print," "Page"	Prints the page.
Press	ALT - =	Displays menu bar.
Select	"File," "Exit"	Displays Save prompt.
Select	"No"	Does not save document.
Select	"No"	Clears screen.

PROCEDURE SUMMARY

SETTING TABS

Activate the menu bar.	ALT - =
Select "Layout."	L

Select "Line."	L
Select "Tab Set."	T or 8
Delete the tab settings.	CTRL-END
Enter the new tab setting.	(your input)
Accept the new tab setting.	↵ ENTER
Return to the document.	F7, F7

CHANGING TABS

Position the cursor at the location for the change.	
Display the Codes screen.	F11
Delete the [Tab Set] code.	DELETE or ←BACKSPACE
Activate the menu bar.	ALT-=
Select "Layout."	L
Select "Line."	L
Select "Tab Set."	T or 8
Delete the tab settings.	CTRL-END
Enter the new tab setting.	(your input)
Accept the new tab setting.	↵ ENTER
Return to the document.	F7, F7

USING DIFFERENT TAB TYPES

Activate the menu bar.	ALT-=
Select "Layout."	L
Select "Line."	L
Select "Tab Set."	T or 8
Delete the tab settings.	CTRL-END
Enter the new tab setting.	(your input)
Accept the new tab setting.	↵ ENTER
Select the tab type.	D or R or C or .
Accept tab setting and type.	↵ ENTER
Return to the document.	F7, F7

EXERCISES

6A Complete the following tasks:

1. Enter a [Tab Set] code with one tab at +0.75". Type the first paragraph below. Press ENTER twice to end it.
2. Enter a new [Tab Set] code with tabs at +0.75" and +1.25". Press TAB once before and once after each asterisk. Press ENTER twice between items.
3. After the last item, press ENTER twice and type the last paragraph.

```
   We are all too busy to accomplish all that we hope in
any one day. It is important then to know what you can do to
become an optimistic, energetic person.

   *   Make friends with nonworriers

   *   Make time for some solitude

   *   Relax your standards; be realistic

   *   Talk it out with a friend

   *   Plan ahead

   *   Do not rely on your memory; write it down

   Keep these simple reminders in mind and you may find
that you gain better control over your time.
```

4. Save your work as EXER6A and leave the document on the screen.
5. Print EXER6A.
6. Exit WordPerfect or complete the next exercise.

6B Complete the following tasks:

1. Retrieve EXER6A. Press PAGE UP to position the cursor at the top of the page. Reveal the codes.
2. Insert a [T/B Mar] code to change to a 2-inch top margin.
3. Position the cursor after the second [Tab Set] code, before the asterisked items.
4. Enter a new [Tab Set] code with tabs at +0.5" and +1".
5. Delete the first [Tab Set] code of these two codes.
6. Remove the Codes screen and view your document.
7. Save EXER6A as a new file named EXER6B. Print a copy.
8. Exit WordPerfect or go on to the next topic.

Changing Line Spacing and Paper Orientation

CONCEPTS Single spacing and regular-size paper are commonly used for business documents. Double spacing may be preferable for the first draft of a report; it is easier to read and edit. You may also have a document that looks best with a combination of single- and double-spaced lines. Some work looks best if it is printed sideways on the paper, for example, a chart with statistical data that will not fit on the regular-size sheet.

Changing the Line Spacing

53

The line spacing can be changed as often as necessary in a document. You can change the line spacing after the document has been typed, too.

To change the line spacing, position the cursor to the location where the new spacing should start. When you change the line spacing, that setting becomes effective for the rest of the document or until you make another change.

Depending on your software, you may not see double-spaced text on the screen. Some packages insert the code to instruct the printer to double-space but to display the text single-spaced on the screen. WordPerfect displays the text double-spaced on the screen.

Changing the Paper Orientation

53

Word processing software has a default paper size and orientation. The default size is 8½ × 11 inches, and the orientation is portrait. Orientation is the way the type runs across the page. If the type runs across the width of the paper (8½" side), the orientation is portrait. If the type appears across the length of the paper (11" side), the orientation is landscape. You might think of landscape printing as sideways printing.

To print sideways, you need to change the paper orientation. The margins may also need to be changed for the wider space. In WordPerfect, you only need to change the paper orientation. The margins are still set at 1 inch, and default tabs are at 0.5-inch intervals across the page.

With a laser printer, the paper is pulled from the same tray and the laser beam prints sideways, as if it were turning its beam in a different direction. On a dot matrix printer, you insert the paper sideways.

TIP Many dot matrix printers have a mechanism by which you can insert a single sheet without disconnecting the feed tractor.

TUTORIAL

In this tutorial, you change TOPIC6 to double spacing. You also change the paper orientation to landscape. WordPerfect should be started. If you need to check and/or change the current directory, do so. Insert your document disk in drive A: to save your work.

1 Change the line spacing.

Press	ALT-=	Displays menu bar.
Select	"File," "Retrieve"	Displays Retrieve prompt.
Type	topic6	Enters filename.
Press	↵ ENTER	Retrieves TOPIC6.
Press	PAGE DOWN	Moves cursor to bottom of page.
Press	ALT-=	Displays menu bar.
Select	"Layout," "Line"	Displays Line Format menu.
Select	"Line Spacing"	Moves cursor to line spacing field.
Type	2	Enters double spacing.
Press	↵ ENTER	Accepts line spacing change.
Press	F7	Returns to document.

TIP You can specify any number (½, .75, 2.25, 3, 4, 10) for line spacing, but your printer must be able to print at the setting. If you type a fraction, WordPerfect converts it to the decimal equivalent.

You can execute the Line Spacing command from the keyboard with the Shift-F8 key. You can click on the right mouse button to return to the document.

Press	F11	Displays [Ln Spacing] code.
Press	F11	Removes Codes screen.
Press	TAB	Indents paragraph.

Type the following paragraph.

```
   Learn what fonts are available for your printer and
choose a font that is appropriate for your document. Common
fonts for text are 10, 11, or 12 point proportional or 10
and 12 cpi. Titles or headings often use 18 or 24 point
fonts or 6 or 8 cpi.
```

Press	↵ ENTER	Ends paragraph.
Press	ALT-=	Displays menu bar.

Select	"File," "Print," "View Document"	Displays View screen.
Press	(SPACEBAR) twice	Returns to document.

2 Change the line spacing and the top margin.

TOPIC6 should be on the screen.

Press	(F11)	Displays Codes screen.

Watch the screen to determine how many times to press the directional arrows to position the cursor on the [Ln Spacing] code.

Press	(↑), (←)	Moves cursor to [Ln Spacing:2] code.
Press	(DELETE)	Deletes code.

The paragraph returns to default single spacing.

Press	(HOME) twice, (↑), (←)	Moves cursor to [T/B Mar:1.5",1"] code.
Press	(DELETE)	Deletes code.

The default top and bottom margins are in effect.

Press	(F11)	Removes Codes screen.
Press	(ALT)-(=)	Displays menu bar.
Select	"File," "Print," "Page"	Prints page.

3 Change the paper orientation.

TOPIC6 should be on the screen.

Press	(HOME) three times, (↑)	Moves cursor to first code on page.

Pressing Home three times and then the Up arrow places the cursor on the first code whether it is text or an electronic code.

Press	(ALT)-(=)	Displays menu bar.
Select	"Layout," "Page"	Displays Page Format menu.
Select	"Paper Size"	Displays Paper Size/Type menu.
Press	(↓)	Highlights "Standard - Wide 11" × 8.5"."

Select	"Select"	Selects new paper size.
Press	F7	Returns to document.

You can execute the Paper Size/Type command from the keyboard with the Shift-F8 key.

Press	F11	Displays [Paper Sz/Typ] code.
Press	ALT-=	Displays menu bar.
Select	"File," "Print," "View Document"	Displays View screen.

The View screen shows the landscape or sideways orientation of the page.

Press	SPACEBAR	Displays Print menu.

If you have a printer with a tractor feed, manually feed the paper sideways.

TIP When you delete format codes such as [Tab Set], [Ln Spacing], or [Paper Sz/Typ], WordPerfect resumes the default settings unless you insert a new code.

Select	"Page"	Prints page.
Press	HOME three times, ↑	Moves cursor to [Paper Sz/Type] code.
Press	DELETE	Deletes code.
Press	ALT-=	Displays menu bar.
Select	"File," "Print," "View Document"	Displays View screen.

The page returns to portrait, 8½" × 11" paper. ◀

Press	SPACEBAR twice	Returns to document.
Press	F11	Removes Codes screen.
Press	ALT-=	Displays menu bar.
Select	"File," "Exit"	Displays Save prompt.
Select	"Yes"	Displays filename.
Press	END	Moves cursor to end of line.
Press	←BACKSPACE	Deletes 6.
Type	7	Enters new filename.
Press	↵ENTER	Saves TOPIC7.
Select	"No"	Clears screen.

PROCEDURE SUMMARY

CHANGING THE LINE SPACING

Position the cursor where the spacing should be changed.	
Activate the menu bar.	ALT-=
Select "Layout."	L
Select "Line."	L
Select "Line Spacing."	S or 6
Enter the new line spacing.	(your input)
Accept the new line spacing.	↵ ENTER
Return to the document.	F7

CHANGING THE PAPER ORIENTATION

Position the cursor at the top of the document.	HOME, HOME, HOME, ↑
Activate the menu bar.	ALT-=
Select "Layout."	L
Select "Page."	P
Select "Paper Size."	S or 7
Highlight the new size.	(your input)
Accept the new size.	S or 1
Return to the document.	F7

EXERCISES

7A Complete the following tasks:

1. Enter a [Tab Set] code with one tab at +0.5". Type the first paragraph of the following text. Press ENTER twice to end it.
2. Before typing the first asterisk, enter a [Ln Spacing] code to change to double spacing. Enter a new [Tab Set] code with tabs at +0.5" and +1". Press TAB once before and once after each asterisk. Press ENTER one time between items.

3. After the last item, press ENTER one time and return to single spacing. Then type the last paragraph.

```
   As you learn about various software packages, you will
find it especially helpful if you are comfortable with DOS.
DOS is the Disk Operating System of your machine and
includes many commands for customizing your computer. DOS
commands which are important include the following.

   *   Change Directory (CD)

   *   Make Directory (MD)

   *   CLS (Clear screen)

   *   FORMAT

   *   DIR (Directory)

   *   ERASE (same as DELETE)

   *   COPY

   *   RENAME

   With a basic understanding of DOS, you will gain better
control over your system. You will also be able to
troubleshoot your own problems more quickly.
```

4. Save your work as EXER7A and leave the document on the screen.
5. Reveal the codes and look for the [Ln Spacing] and the [Tab Set] codes. Remove the Codes screen.
6. Print EXER7A.

7. Exit WordPerfect or complete the next exercise.

7B Complete the following the tasks:

1. Retrieve EXER4A. Position the cursor at the top of the page and reveal the codes.
2. Change to 11 × 8½-inch wide paper. The [Paper Sz/Typ] code should be the first code in the document. If it is not, delete it, reposition the cursor, and insert it again.
3. Change to a 2-inch top margin after the [Paper Sz/Typ] code.
4. Change to double spacing after the [T/B Mar] code.
5. Remove the Codes screen and view your document.
6. Save EXER4A as a new file named EXER7B. Print a copy.
7. Exit WordPerfect or go on to the next topic.

Checkpoint 1

What You Should Know

- ✓ WordPerfect has pull-down menus for command selection and keyboard commands. You can use either or any combination of both. The mouse can be used to position the cursor or to make selections from a menu.
- ✓ WordPerfect has 1-inch default left, right, top, and bottom margins. Default tabs are set at 0.5-inch intervals across the page. The default paper size is 8½ × 11. Margins, tabs, line spacing, and paper orientation can be changed by inserting the necessary codes.
- ✓ WordPerfect operates in an insert mode so that any characters that you type are added to the existing document. You can delete characters with the DELETE key or the BACKSPACE key. There are also shortcuts to delete a word and a line.
- ✓ A document must be saved to disk if you need to refer to it at a later time.
- ✓ Files are retrieved by typing the name of the document at the Retrieve prompt or by listing the files to the screen.
- ✓ When documents are edited, they should be resaved using either the same name or a new name. If you use the same name, the original file is replaced.
- ✓ Codes can be deleted or inserted. WordPerfect codes are visible when you reveal the codes. The Codes screen is helpful when you are trying to determine if something is wrong or when you are adding and deleting codes.
- ✓ WordPerfect must be exited properly to avoid damage to the software and documents.

Review Questions

1. How do you start WordPerfect?
2. How do you display the menu bar?
3. How do you make a selection from the menu bar?
4. How do you exit WordPerfect?
5. What are the steps to save a document?
6. Why might you need to list the files?
7. What key changes to the Typeover mode?
8. What happens to the original file when you resave a file with the same name? With a new name?
9. What is the command to view a document?
10. From what three locations can you print a document?

11. How do you reveal or display the electronic codes?
12. What are the default margin settings?
13. How do you print sideways on the paper?
14. Which menu option is used to change tab settings?
15. What are two alignment choices for tab settings?

CHECKPOINT PROBLEM A

1. Enter a [T/B Mar] code to change the top margin to 1.5 inches. Then type the return address, the inside address, the salutation, and the first paragraph.
2. Before starting the listed items, enter a new [Tab Set] code to clear the default tabs and set one tab 0.5 inch from the margin and a second tab 2 inches from the margin.
3. Enter a [Ln Spacing] code to change to double spacing.
4. Before typing the last paragraph, enter another [Ln Spacing] code to return to single spacing for the remainder of the letter.
5. Proofread your work and save it as CKPT1A.
6. View your work and ~~print a copy~~.

```
Your Street Address
Your City, State ZIP
Today's Date

Mr. Thomas Wilkins
3344 South West End Boulevard
San Mateo, CA 92310-3344

Dear Mr. Wilkins:

You will be pleased to learn that we will be conducting
training sessions in the San Mateo area. The dates and top-
ics are listed here.

   January 5     WordPerfect 5.1

   January 12    dBASE III PLUS

   January 19    Lotus 1-2-3

If you or your staff are interested in enrolling, please
call my office at 555-212-1212 as soon as you can.

Sincerely yours,


Your Name
President

xx/ckpt1a
```

CHECKPOINT PROBLEM B

1. Enter a [Paper Sz/Typ] code to change to a landscape or wide orientation.
2. Enter a [T/B Mar] code to change the top margin to 2 inches.
3. Enter a [Ln Spacing] code to change to 1.5 spacing.
4. Enter a [L/R Mar] code to change to 2-inch left and right margins.
5. Enter a [Tab Set] code to set one tab at or near the center of the page (5.5 inches from the edge of the page or 3.5 inches from the left margin). Tabs are figured from the margin, not from the edge of the page. A tab set at +3.5" appears at 5.5" on the page because your left margin is now 2".
6. Check the codes for [Paper Sz/Typ], [T/B Mar], [Ln Spacing], [L/R Mar], and [Tab Set]. If any codes are missing or incorrect, position the cursor and insert them. Delete unnecessary or wrong codes.
7. Type the first line of the document and view your work. If you are not satisfied with the tab setting, reveal the codes and position the cursor to change the [Tab Set] code. Insert the new code and delete the old one.
8. Type the remaining items.
9. Save your work as CKPT1B. View it and print a copy.

```
SHORTCUT                 RESULT
Ctrl/Down                Cursor moves to next paragraph.
Ctrl/Up                  Cursor moves to previous paragraph.
Ctrl/Left                Cursor moves to previous word.
Ctrl/Right               Cursor moves to next word.
Ctrl/Backspace           Deletes a word.
Ctrl/End                 Deletes a line.
Page Up                  Cursor moves to top of page.
Page Down                Cursor moves to bottom of page.
```

Changing the Appearance of Text

CONCEPTS Underline and bold add emphasis to text. Side headings in a report might use a bigger type size to mark each new section. Underline is used to show totals or subtotals. Important words in a report can be italic so that the reader spots them quickly. If you print on shaded paper, you can also use bold print so that the print is more prominent.

TIP It is accepted practice to not underline punctuation. If words at the end of a sentence are underlined, the underline should stop just before the period.

Using Underline or Bold

65

Underline and bold are usually simple commands. You can apply the underline style as you type. Most word processing software also have a way to add underline or bold to text that is already typed.

Underlined text prints with a single line. Your software may also have an option for a double underline. Bold text appears darker on the printed page than normal text. On the screen you may not see underline or bold, depending on the type of monitor you use. Text that has a special style may appear in reverse video, highlighted, or in a different color. ◀

Styles that can be applied to text can be removed when they are no longer needed. If you type a document with underlined titles and then decide they should be bold, you can remove the underlining and change to bold.

Using Italic or Other Styles

65

TIP Your software may offer italic or small caps as options, but the printer cannot do it. Most printers print the text with whatever style is available. You could, for example, use italic in the software but see underline on the printed page.

Most published materials such as newspapers or books use italic in place of underline. Like underline and bold, italic is used for emphasis or to show a division of the text. Bold italic can be used for a prominent title line.

Other text styles that are common to word processors are shadow printing, strikeover, redline, small caps, and outline. Shadow printing is similar to bold, but the characters are slightly offset from one another. Strikeover places a vertical or diagonal line through the character to show that it has been changed from an original document. Redline is an editor's tool for marking text that has been changed. Sometimes this is a mark in the margin, or the characters are displayed with a shaded background. Small caps are little capital letters, and outline characters show a hollow silhouette of the letter. Your software may have these options, or it may have other text styles. ◀

Using Fonts (65)

A font is the typeface, size, and style of the characters. Fonts have names like Times, Courier, and Line Printer. When you change the font, you use a different design of character.

Fonts add variety to the page. Titles in a newspaper, for example, are printed in a larger font than the column. Page numbers generally use a smaller font. By learning to use fonts correctly, you can add a professional appearance to your work.

Fonts can be software files stored on disk. Some fonts are stored in the printer's RAM. Fonts can also be kept on a cartridge which you insert into the printer. Regardless of where the fonts are located, WordPerfect must be installed to recognize and use the fonts. ◀

> **TIP** Do not use more than two fonts or typefaces per page. You can use different styles of the font such as bold, bold italic, or underline for variety.

TUTORIAL

In this tutorial, you type and save a document using bold, underline, and italic. You also use at least one of the other fonts available at your printer. Change the current directory if necessary, and insert your document disk in drive A: to save your work.

1 Use underline and bold.

Press	F8	Starts Underline.
Type	CPU	Underlines characters.

The word appears underlined, in a different color, or in reverse video, depending on your monitor. The number after "Pos" in the status line changes to the same display used for the underline style.

Press	F11	Displays [UND] and [und] codes.

The [UND] code starts the underline, and the [und] code ends it as shown in Figure 8.1.

Press	F8	Moves cursor to right of [und] code.

Underline is canceled when the cursor is past the ending [und] code. Leave the codes revealed as you continue.

Press	SPACEBAR	Inserts space.

Type the following text.

```
is an acronym for Central Processing Unit. It is the computer's
processor chip, the
```

Figure 8.1
TOPIC8 with Underline Codes

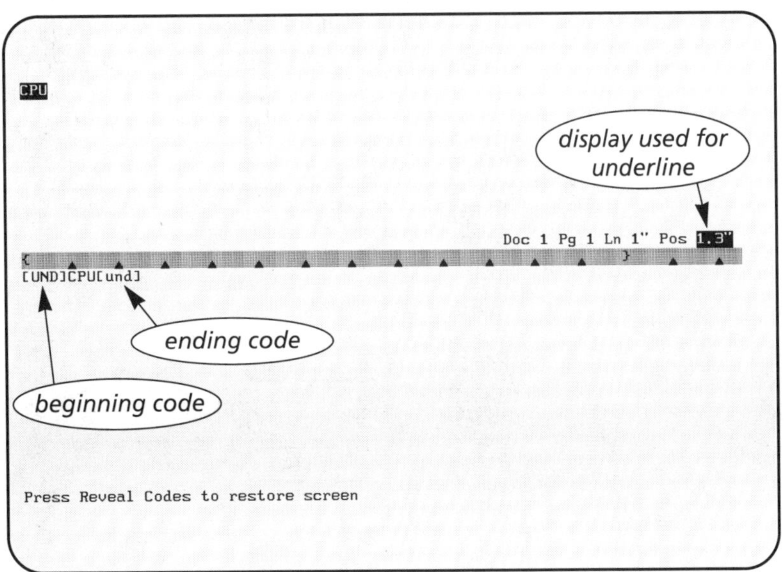

Press	SPACEBAR	Inserts space.
Press	F6	Starts Bold.

When you start bold or underline, both codes are inserted. The cursor is positioned so that what you type is between the codes.

Type	brain	Bolds word.

The word appears in a different color or in reverse video. The number after "Pos" changes to the display used for the bold style.

TIP You can cancel Bold or Underline by pressing F6 or F8 or by pressing the RIGHT arrow one time.

Press	F6	Cancels Bold.

The [BOLD] code starts bold, and the [bold] code ends it. Bold is canceled when the cursor is past the ending [bold] code. ◀

Press	SPACEBAR	Inserts space.
Type	of the machine.	Finishes sentence.
Press	↵ ENTER twice	Ends paragraph.
Press	F8	Starts Underline.
Type	Disk Drive	Underlines space and words.
Press	→	Moves cursor to right of [und] code.
Press	SPACEBAR	Inserts space.

Type the following text.

```
is the physical device that allows the computer to read or write
data from a disk. Disk drives are either
```

Press	SPACEBAR	Inserts space.
Press	F6	Starts Bold.
Type	hard	Bolds word.
Press	→	Cancels Bold.
Press	SPACEBAR	Inserts space.
Type	or	Inserts a word without Bold.
Press	SPACEBAR	Inserts space.
Press	F6	Starts Bold.
Type	floppy	Bolds word.
Press	F6	Cancels Bold.
Type	.	Ends sentence.
Press	↵ ENTER twice	Ends paragraph.

TIP Watch the upper window; it is less confusing.

2 **Remove underline and bold.** The paragraphs from Task 1 should be on the screen with the codes revealed. ◀

Press	PAGE UP	Moves cursor to top of page.

The cursor should be on the [UND] code in the Codes screen.

Press	DELETE	Deletes [UND] code.

To remove a style (underline, bold, or italics), you only need to delete one code of the pair. You may delete either code. Watch the screen to determine how many times to press the directional arrows and Control-Left or Control-Right to position the cursor on the [BOLD] code before "brain."

Press	↓, CTRL-→, CTRL-←	Moves cursor to [BOLD] code.
Press	DELETE	Deletes [BOLD] code.
Press	PAGE DOWN	Moves cursor to bottom of page.

3 **Use italic and redline.** The paragraphs from Tasks 1 and 2 should be on the screen with the codes revealed. Beginning with this topic, the directions only show the selection of menu commands. You know now that you need to display the menu by pressing ALT and the = key.

Select	"Font"	Displays Font menu.
Select	"Appearance"	Displays Appearance menu.
Select	"Italics"	Starts Italics.
Type	RAM	Italicizes word.
Press	→	Moves cursor past [italc] code.

TIP Bold and Underline are listed in the Appearance menu. They can be used more quickly, however, from the keyboard.

You can execute the Font Appearance command from the keyboard with the Ctrl-F8 key.

Press	SPACEBAR	Inserts space.

Type the following sentence.

```
is an acronym for random access memory that stores data only
temporarily.
```

Press	↵ ENTER twice	Ends paragraph.
Select	"Font," "Appearance"	Displays Appearance menu.
Select	"Redline"	Starts Redline.
Type	ROM	Redlines word.
Press	→	Cancels Redline.
Press	SPACEBAR	Inserts space.

TIP If your printer does not support italic or redline, the text may be underlined. To see what your printer capabilities are, you can print out the PRINTER.TST document that is provided with the software.

Type the following text.

```
is an acronym for read only memory that is burned into a computer
chip. ROM cannot be erased.
```

Press	↵ ENTER twice	Ends paragraph.
Select	"File," "Print," "Page"	Prints page.

The page prints with the styles that your printer can do.

4 **Change font size.** The paragraphs from Tasks 1, 2, and 3 should be on the screen with the codes revealed.

Select	"Font"	Displays Font menu.
Select	"Fine"	Starts Fine size.

Type the following sentence.

```
There are a variety of printers on the market.
```

Press	→	Moves cursor past [fine] code.
Press	SPACEBAR twice	Inserts two spaces.

Select	"Font," "Large"	Starts Large size.

Type the following sentence.

```
The major categories are LaserJet, PostScript, dot matrix,
printwheel, thermal transfer, and ink jet.
```

Press	→	Moves cursor past [large] code.
Press	SPACEBAR twice	Inserts two spaces.
Select	"Font," "Extra Large"	Starts Extra Large size.

Type the following sentence.

```
Suitability to printing objectives, rather than cost, should be
the determining factor.
```

Press	→	Moves cursor past [ext large] code.

The default font size is resumed. Type the following sentence.

```
Before selecting a printer, check the print quality, speed,
printing features, and compatibility.
```

Press	↵ ENTER twice	Ends paragraph.
Select	"File," "Print," "View Document"	Displays View screen.
Type	1	Displays print-size view.
Press	F7	Returns to document.
Select	"File," "Save"	Displays Save prompt.
Type	topic8	Enters filename.
Press	↵ ENTER	Saves TOPIC8.

5 **Change the base font.** TOPIC8 should be on the screen with the Codes screen revealed.

Select	"Font," "Base Font"	Displays your printer's fonts.

Your default base font is highlighed and marked with an asterisk. Select a different font from your list.

Select	(your input)	Highlights a different font.
Select	"Select"	Displays font code.

> **TIP** When you change the Base Font, there is no ending font code as there is with Font Size or Appearance. The new font is in effect until you enter another font code.

Type the following sentence.

```
CGA, EGA, and VGA are three types of color monitors.
```

You can execute the Base Font command from the keyboard with the Ctrl-F8 key. ◀

Select	"File," "Print," "View Document"	Displays View screen.
Press	SPACEBAR	Displays Print menu.
Select	"Page"	Prints page.
Press	F11	Removes Codes screen.
Select	"File," "Exit," "Yes"	Displays "Document to be saved: A:\TOPIC8."
Press	↵ ENTER	Displays "Replace A:\TOPIC8?"
Select	"Yes"	Replaces TOPIC8.
Select	"No"	Clears screen.

PROCEDURE SUMMARY

USING UNDERLINE OR BOLD

Start Underline or Bold.	F8 or F6
Type the text.	(your input)
End Underline or Bold.	F8 or F6 or →
Delete underline or bold.	
Position cursor on beginning or ending code.	DELETE

USING ITALIC OR OTHER STYLES

Start Italic.	
Activate the menu bar.	ALT-=
Select "Font," "Appearance," "Italics."	O, A, I
Type the text.	(your input)
End Italic.	→

USING FONTS

To change the font size:

Activate the menu bar.	ALT-=
Select "Font."	O
Select the size.	(your input)

Type the text.	(your input)
End the size.	→

To change the base font:

Activate the menu bar.	ALT-=
Select "Font," "Base Font."	O, O
Highlight a new font name.	(your input)
Choose the new font.	1 or S

EXERCISES

8A Complete the following tasks:

1. Enter a [Tab Set] code with one tab at +2".
2. Press ENTER six times to add more space to the top margin without a [T/B Mar] code.
3. Change to double spacing after the six hard returns.
4. Start underline and type "MENU" at the left margin. Press TAB, type "OPTIONS" as the second title. Turn off underline. Press ENTER.
5. Use italic or bold for the words in the first column. Start bold or italic and type the word. Turn off bold or italic. Press TAB and type the data in the second column. Repeat these steps for each line.

```
MENU        OPTIONS
File        Retrieve, Print, List Files, Save, Exit
Edit        Undelete, Reveal Codes
Layout      Line, Page
Font        Base Font, Appearance, Size
Help        Help, Index, Template
```

6. Reveal the codes and check your work. Remove the Codes screen and view the document. Print a copy of your work.
7. Save your work as EXER8A. Exit WordPerfect or complete the next exercise.

8B Complete the following tasks:

1. Retrieve EXER6A. With the cursor at the top of the page, reveal the codes.
2. As the first code in the document, enter a [Font] code to change to a font different from your default base font.
3. Remove the Codes screen and view your document. Print a copy.
4. Clear the screen without resaving EXER6A.
5. Exit WordPerfect or go on to the next topic.

Using Blocks of Text

CONCEPTS

You might need to save three or four paragraphs from one document to use in another document. Maybe you need to delete five paragraphs or five pages from a 100-page report. Parts of a document are blocks of text. Being able to identify blocks of text allows you to work more efficiently. It is quicker to block three paragraphs to be deleted than it is to delete each paragraph separately.

Defining a Block of Text

72

To identify a block of text, you need to position the cursor at the first character in the block. Then you highlight up to and including the last character in the block. Highlighting means that the text is shaded or displayed in reverse video. A Block command simply marks text for your next activity.

When highlighting or blocking text, you can use regular cursor movement commands to shade the desired portion. To highlight three paragraphs, for example, press ENTER three times. To block a page, use the PAGE DOWN key. You can usually identify a block by dragging the mouse across it or by clicking at each end of the block. The arrow keys can be used to trim highlighting if you block too much. Of course, you can cancel the Block command if you change your mind.

> **TIP** You can use the Block command to bold or underline text that has already been typed. Other features that can be used with Block include capitalization, centering, moving, and copying.

Deleting a Block

72

You can delete groups of sentences, paragraphs, or pages. If you want to delete three sentences, you can use the Block command to mark the text so that only one Delete command is necessary. A block of text is deleted by giving the regular Delete command. This allows you to make major corrections or revisions without the need for individual Delete commands.

Saving a Block

72

If you work for a company that uses the same closing paragraph for all letters, you can save that paragraph as a block and retrieve it. You save typing time and proofreading time as long as your original block is correct.

A block of text can be saved as a permanent file with a name. A block saved as a permanent file is retrieved like any document. WordPerfect also allows you to save a block as a temporary file, which is deleted when you exit the software.

> **TIP** To print a block, highlight the text and give the Print command. A printed block prints in the same position on the page that it would if the entire page had been printed.

Printing a Block

73

You can print a portion of the page by identifying it as a block. Maybe you have downloaded a document from an electronic bulletin board and find that only a few paragraphs are important to you. You can highlight those paragraphs and print them faster than the whole page. ◀

TUTORIAL In this tutorial, you retrieve a document and use the Block command. You delete and save a block of text and apply bold and underline to blocked text. Change the current directory if necessary, and insert your document disk in drive A: to save your work. The directions only show the selection of menu commands.

1 Highlight blocks.

Select	"File," "Retrieve"	Displays Retrieve prompt.
Type	ckpt1a	Enters filename.
Press	↵ENTER	Retrieves CKPT1A.
Select	"Edit"	Displays Edit menu.
Select	"Block"	Flashes "Block on."
Press	SPACEBAR	Blocks one word.
Press	SPACEBAR three times	Blocks three more words.
Press	↵ENTER	Blocks to hard return.
Type	:	Blocks to colon.
Type	S (uppercase)	Blocks to the "S" in "San Mateo."
Press	F1	Cancels Block.

Block starts from the current cursor position. Text is highlighted up to and including whatever key you press. If you press any alphanumeric character or format key (Tab or Enter), text is highlighted up to the first occurrence of that character or code. You can execute the Block command from the keyboard with the F12 key or the ALT-F4 key.

Select	"Edit," "Block"	Flashes "Block on."
Press	↵ENTER twice	Blocks to second hard return.

The second hard return is at the end of the paragraph.

Press	PAGE DOWN	Blocks remainder of page.
Press	F1	Cancels Block.

2 **Delete a block.**
CKPT1A should be on the screen.

Press	PAGE UP	Moves cursor to top of page.
Select	"Edit," "Block"	Flashes "Block on."
Press	↵ ENTER three times	Blocks three lines ending with hard returns.
Press	DELETE	Displays "Delete Block?"
Select	"Yes"	Deletes block.
Select	"Edit," "Undelete," "Restore"	Restores lines.

TIP CTRL-DOWN or CTRL-UP moves the cursor up or down by paragraphs on an enhanced keyboard. On a standard keyboard, use the UP or DOWN arrow.

You can execute the Undelete command from the keyboard with the F1 key. Watch the screen to determine how many times to press Control-Down to move the cursor to "If" in the last paragraph. ◀

Press	CTRL-↓	Moves cursor to "I" in "If."
Select	"Edit," "Block"	Flashes "Block on."
Press	↵ ENTER twice	Blocks paragraph and two returns.
Press	DELETE	Displays "Delete Block?"
Select	"Yes"	Deletes block.
Select	"Edit," "Undelete," "Restore"	Restores lines.

TIP When you block backwards, you can only use cursor movement shortcuts. You cannot type a character to highlight up to that letter.

3 **Save a block as a file.** Watch the screen to determine how many times to press the Up Arrow to move the cursor to the "Lotus 1-2-3" line. ◀

Press	↑, END	Moves cursor to end of "Lotus 1-2-3."
Select	"Edit," "Block"	Flashes "Block on."
Press	↑ three times	Blocks date and topic lines.
Select	"File," "Save"	Displays "Block name."
Type	topic9	Enters filename.
Press	↵ ENTER	Saves block as TOPIC9.
Select	"File," "Exit," "No," "No"	Clears screen.

Select	"File," "List Files"	Displays directory name.
Press	↵ ENTER	Lists files.
Select	TOPIC9	Highlights filename.
Select	"Retrieve"	Retrieves TOPIC9.
Select	"File," "Exit," "No," "No"	Clears screen.

4 Save a block as a temporary file.

Select	"File," "Retrieve"	Displays Retrieve prompt.
Type	ckpt1a	Enters filename.
Press	↵ ENTER	Retrieves CKPT1A.
Press	F11	Displays Codes screen.

Watch the screen to determine how many times to press the Down Arrow to position the cursor on the [Tab] code before "January 5."

Press	↓	Moves cursor to first [Tab] code.
Press	F11	Removes Codes screen.
Select	"Edit," "Block"	Flashes "Block on."
Press	↵ ENTER three times	Blocks three lines ending with [HRt].
Select	"File," "Save"	Displays "Block name."
Press	↵ ENTER	Saves block without a name.
Press	PAGE DOWN	Moves cursor to bottom of page.
Press	↵ ENTER twice	Inserts two hard returns.
Select	"File," "Retrieve"	Displays "Document to be retrieved."
Press	↵ ENTER	Retrieves unnamed file.

TIP A temporary, unnamed file is accessible until you exit WordPerfect. When you exit, the file is deleted from memory.

The second copy of the table is single spaced because it assumes the line spacing in effect at the end of the letter. ◀

Select	"File," "List Files"	Displays directory name.
Press	↵ ENTER	Lists files.

You can list the files to the screen while a document is displayed. The temporary file has no filename.

Press	SPACEBAR	Removes list.

The cursor should be positioned at Pos 1" before "January 5" in the retrieved block.

Press	CTRL-PAGE DOWN	Displays "Delete Remainder of page?"
Select	"Yes"	Deletes block.

5 **Add underline and bold to a block.** Watch the screen to determine how many times to press the Up Arrow and Control-Right to move the cursor to the "y" in "you" in the first line of the last paragraph.

Press	↑, CTRL-→	Moves cursor to "y" in "you."
Select	"Edit," "Block"	Flashes "Block on."
Press	SPACEBAR four times	Blocks four words.
Press	←	Trims block so space is not included.
Press	F8	Underlines block.

Determine how many times to press the Down Arrow and Control-Left to move the cursor to the "P" in "President" below your name.

Press	↓, CTRL-←	Moves cursor to "P" in "President."
Select	"Edit," "Block"	Flashes "Block on."
Press	↵ ENTER	Blocks line.
Press	F6	Bolds "President."

6 **Add capitalization to a block.** Watch the screen to determine how many times to press Control-Up to move the cursor to the "J" in "January 5."

Press	CTRL-↑	Moves cursor to "J."
Select	"Edit," "Block"	Flashes "Block on."
Press	↵ ENTER three times	Blocks three lines.
Select	"Edit," "Convert Case"	Displays Convert Case menu.

> **TIP** If you try to select Convert Case without having defined a block, the option in the menu appears in brackets [ ] to show that it is unavailable. If you press Shift-F3 with no block defined, you switch to Doc 2. Press Shift-F3 again to return to Doc 1.

Convert Case is available only after a block has been defined. You can change to uppercase or lowercase letters.

Select	"To Upper"	Converts lines to uppercase letters.

You can execute the Convert Case command from the keyboard with the Shift-F3 key. ◀

Select	"File," "Exit," "No," "No"	Clears screen.

PROCEDURE SUMMARY

DEFINING A BLOCK OF TEXT

Position the cursor at the first character.	
Activate the menu bar.	ALT - =
Select "Edit," "Block."	E, B
Highlight the desired amount of text.	(your input)

DELETING A BLOCK

Position the cursor at the first character.	
Activate the menu bar.	ALT - =
Select "Edit," "Block."	E, B
Highlight the desired amount of text.	(your input)
Delete the block.	DELETE
Respond to "Delete Block?"	Y

SAVING A BLOCK

Position the cursor at the first character.	
Activate the menu bar.	ALT - =
Select "Edit," "Block."	E, B
Highlight the desired amount of text.	(your input)
Activate the menu bar.	ALT - =
Select "File," "Save."	F, S
Type filename if desired.	(your input)
Save block.	↵ ENTER

PRINTING A BLOCK

Position the cursor at the first character.	
Activate the menu bar.	ALT-=
Select "Edit," "Block."	E, B
Highlight the desired amount of text.	(your input)
Activate the menu bar.	ALT-=
Select "File," "Print."	F, P
Respond to "Print Block?"	Y

EXERCISES

9A Complete the following tasks:

1. Type the following document. Type the title at the left margin. Press ENTER three times after it.

```
Hard Disk Problems
   Users have a tendency to expect their hard disk computers to
work without a hitch. Unfortunately, that is not always the
case.
   Hard disks can fail for a number of reasons. As a disk is
used repeatedly, it is likely to develop surface defects. The
alignment of the read/write heads can drift, too. Combine these
two common problems and you might see the message "Abort, Retry,
or Fail?"
   A PC service organization can run diagnostic tests and
alert you to potential problems. There are also many utilities
programs available that perform the same service at considerably
less cost.
```

#1

2. Change to 1.5 spacing after the three hard returns.
3. Press TAB to indent the first line of each paragraph.
4. Save your document as EXER9A. Print a copy.
5. Exit WordPerfect or complete the next exercise.

9B Complete the following tasks:

1. Retrieve EXER9A.
2. Block the title and change it to uppercase.
3. Block the phrase "surface defects" in the second paragraph. Type a period to highlight the block and then trim back the highlighting so that the period is not included. Apply Bold to the block.
4. Block the phrase "at considerably less cost" at the end of the document. Trim the block so that the period is not included. Apply Underline to the block.
5. Block the second paragraph and print it.
6. Resave the document as EXER9B and print a copy.
7. Exit WordPerfect or go on to the next topic.

Cursor to Hard F12 →
Edit / convert / upper case

Cursor to Hard 2nd P back up to tab
block + print

Moving and Copying Text

> **TIP** A buffer is a separate part of the machine's memory used to store text or codes that result from certain operations. WordPerfect sets up these buffers each time you start the software and deletes buffers when you exit the software.

> **TIP** You can move or copy text to a different document with the Switch Document command (EDIT, SWITCH DOCUMENT, or SHIFT/F3). Retrieve one document into Doc 1. Switch to Doc 2 and retrieve a second document. Complete the move or copy as usual but switch to the other document before you press ENTER to retrieve the text.

CONCEPTS As you write a letter or a report, you may decide that some sentences or paragraphs might be more effective if they were in a different location. WordPerfect allows you to move or copy text from one location in a document to another. Copying allows you to repeat sentences, phrases, or paragraphs without the need to retype. This saves typing time and proofreading time. Move and Copy allow last-minute changes without the need for retyping.

Moving Text

80

A Move command is a combination delete/insert procedure. The amount of text to be moved is selected or highlighted. When you give the Move command, the text is removed from the screen, and the screen is rewritten as if the text had been deleted. The moved text is stored in a buffer memory until you retrieve it in its new location. ◄

Before you retrieve the moved text, position the cursor where the text should be. This new location might be somewhere else on the same page, on a different page, or maybe in a different document. When the cursor is positioned, you give the command to retrieve the text. The text appears in its new position, and the document is adjusted as if the text had been inserted.

You can usually move specific amounts of text like a sentence, a paragraph, and a page. You can move any amount of text by combining the Move command with the Block command.

Copying Text

80

A Copy command is like a duplicate and paste procedure. Like the Move command, you need to identify the amount of text to be copied. When you give the Copy command, the text stays in its original location and is duplicated in the buffer memory until you retrieve the copy in its new location.

Before you retrieve the copied text, position the cursor in a new location on the same page, on a different page, or in a different document. When the cursor is positioned, give the command to retrieve the copied text from the buffer memory in its new position. ◄

Appending Text

81

If you typed part of a report at school and your friend typed his or her part at home, you can combine your two files by appending one to the other. An Append command copies text from one document to a different

TIP An Append command is one way of combining documents. In WordPerfect, you can also retrieve one document into another to combine them.

document. The steps are similar to copying because you identify the amount to be appended and give the Append command. The text is stored in the buffer memory until you indicate the name of the file to which you want the text added.

An append procedure is a copy/attach process. When you append text, it is added at the end of the receiving document. You could then move it or copy it to wherever you prefer in that document. The original document is not affected because its text is copied to the receiving document. The text is appended to the target document, and this is the file that is changed. ◀

TUTORIAL

In this tutorial, you move or copy a sentence, a paragraph, a page, and a block of text. You also append a block of text to another document. Change the current directory if necessary, and insert your document disk in drive A: to save your work.

1 Move a paragraph.

Select	"File," "Retrieve"	Displays Retrieve prompt.
Type	exer9a	Enters filename.
Press	↵ ENTER	Retrieves EXER9A.
Press	↓ three times	Moves cursor to first paragraph.
Press	F11	Displays cursor on [Tab] code.
Press	←BACKSPACE	Deletes [Ln Spacing:1.5] code.

The paragraphs return to single spacing.

Press	F11	Removes Codes screen.
Select	"Edit"	Displays Edit menu.

Your first need to select the amount to be moved.

Select	"Select"	Displays Select menu.

Five choices appear as shown in Figure 10.1; options in brackets [ ] are unavailable.

Select	"Paragraph"	Blocks paragraph.

The prompt is "1 Move; 2 Copy; 3 Delete; 4 Append:"

Select	"Move"	Moves paragraph to buffer memory.

Figure 10.1
Edit Menu with Select Pull-down Menu

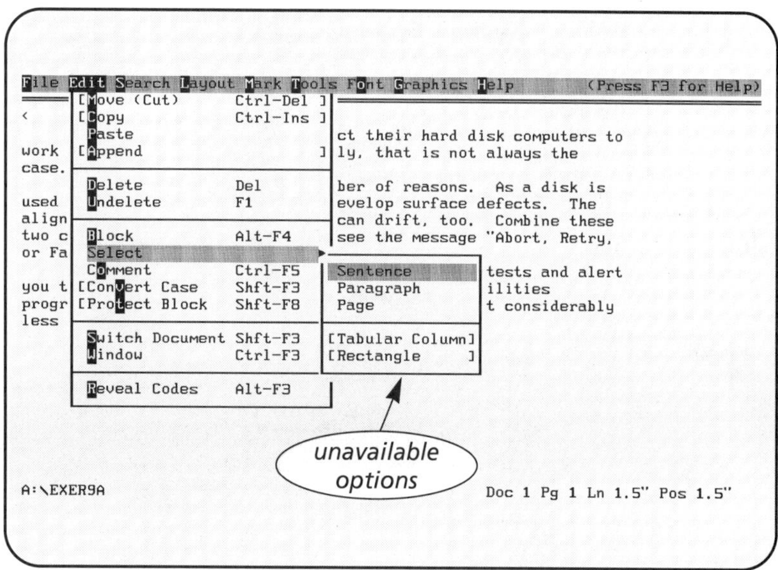

The prompt is "Move cursor; press Enter to retrieve."

Press	PAGE DOWN	Moves cursor to bottom of page.
Press	↵ ENTER	Retrieves paragraph.

You can execute the Move command from the keyboard with the Ctrl-F4 key.

Select	"Edit," "Select," "Paragraph"	Blocks paragraph.
Select	"Move"	Moves paragraph to buffer memory.
Press	PAGE UP	Moves cursor to top of page.
Press	↓ three times	Moves cursor to first paragraph.
Press	↵ ENTER	Retrieves paragraph in its original location.

2 **Move a sentence.** Watch the screen to determine how many times to press the Down Arrow to move the cursor to the beginning of the second paragraph.

Press	↓	Moves cursor to second paragraph.
Select	"Edit," "Select," "Sentence"	Blocks sentence.

The prompt is "1 Move; 2 Copy; 3 Delete; 4 Append:"

Select	"Move"	Moves sentence to buffer memory.

The prompt is "Move cursor; press Enter to retrieve."

Press	↓ three times	Moves cursor to last line of paragraph.
Press	END	Moves cursor to end of paragraph.
Press	↵ ENTER	Retrieves sentence.
Press	SPACEBAR twice	Inserts two spaces.
Select	"Edit," "Select," "Sentence"	Blocks sentence.
Select	"Move"	Displays Move/Retrieve prompt.

Watch the screen to determine how many times to press the Up Arrow and Control-Left to move the cursor to the "A" in "As." The cursor should be after the [Tab] code.

Press	↑, CTRL-←	Moves cursor to "A."
Press	↵ ENTER	Retrieves sentence.

3 Copy a page.

Select	"Edit," "Select," "Page"	Blocks page.

The prompt is "1 Move; 2 Copy; 3 Delete; 4 Append:"

Select	"Copy"	Copies page to buffer memory.

The cursor is at the bottom of the copied page.

Press	↵ ENTER	Copies page.
Press	↑, ↓	Scrolls two copies.

Watch the screen to determine if you need to press the Up or Down Arrows to position the cursor at the beginning of the second title.

Press	↑ or ↓	Moves cursor to second title.

Press	CTRL-PAGE DOWN	Displays "Delete Remainder of page?"
Select	"Yes"	Deletes duplicate page.

4 Copy a block.

> **TIP** The Block/Copy shortcut is CTRL-INS. The Block/Move shortcut is CTRL-DEL. Give these commands after the text is blocked. They work only on an enhanced keyboard.

Press	PAGE UP	Moves cursor to top of page.
Select	"Edit," "Block"	Flashes "Block on."
Press	END	Blocks line.
Press	CTRL-INSERT	Copies block to buffer memory.

Control-Insert is a shortcut for Edit/Copy from the menu. The prompt is "Move cursor; press Enter to retrieve." ◀

Press	PAGE DOWN	Moves cursor to bottom of page.
Press	↵ ENTER	Retrieves title.

5 Append a block.

Select	"Edit," "Block"	Flashes "Block on."

Watch the screen to determine how many times to press the Up Arrow to block the last two paragraphs.

> **TIP** If you enter a filename that does not exist in response to "Append to:", WordPerfect creates a file with that name. Format codes in the block are also appended to the file. If there are no format codes, the appended block uses the format of the file to which it is appended.

Press	↑	Blocks last two paragraphs.
Select	"Edit," "Append"	Displays Append menu.

There are two Append options: "To File" or "To Clipboard." The Clipboard is a part of WordPerfect's Office software package. It allows you to transfer information between different software packages.

Select	"To File"	Displays "Append to."
Type	exer7a	Enters filename.

This is the file to which the copy will be appended. ◀

Press	↵ ENTER	Appends block to EXER7A.
Select	"File," "Exit," "No," "No"	Clears screen.
Select	"File," "Retrieve"	Displays Retrieve prompt.

Type	exer7a	Enters filename.
Press	↵ ENTER	Retrieves EXER7A.

Watch the screen to determine how many times to press the Down Arrow to position the cursor at the beginning of the appended block.

Press	↓	Moves cursor to appended block.
Press	CTRL - PAGE DOWN	Displays "Delete Remainder of page?"
Select	"Yes"	Deletes text.
Select	"File," "Exit," "Yes"	Displays Save prompt.
Press	↵ ENTER	Displays Replace prompt.
Select	"Yes"	Replaces EXER7A.
Select	"No"	Clears screen.

PROCEDURE SUMMARY

MOVING TEXT

Position the cursor at the beginning of the text to be moved.	
Activate the menu bar.	ALT - =
Select "Edit," "Select."	E, E
Select the amount to be moved.	S or P or A
Select the Move option.	M or 1
Move the cursor to the new location.	(your input)
Retrieve text.	↵ ENTER

COPYING TEXT

Position the cursor at the beginning of the text to be copied.	
Activate the menu bar.	ALT - =
Select "Edit," "Select."	E, E
Select the amount to be copied.	S or P or A

Select the Copy option.	C or 2
Move the cursor to the new location.	(your input)
Retrieve text.	↵ ENTER

APPENDING TEXT

Position the cursor at the beginning of the text to be appended.	
Activate the menu bar.	ALT-=
Select "Edit," "Block."	E, B
Highlight the desired amount of text.	(your input)
Activate the menu bar.	ALT-=
Select "Edit," "Append," "To File."	E, A, F
Type the name of the file to which the block is to be appended or a new filename.	(your input)
Append the text.	↵ ENTER

EXERCISES

10A Complete the following tasks:

1. Type the following document. Enter a [Tab Set] code with one tab at +2".

```
Search      Forward, Backward, Go To
Mark        Index, Define, Generate
Tools       Spell, Thesaurus, Date Text
Graphics    Figure, Equation, Line
```

2. Use italic or bold for the words in the first column. Start bold or italic and type the word. Turn off bold or italic after the word. Press TAB and type the data in the second column.
3. Press ENTER one time after the last item.
4. Save your document as EXER10A.
5. Block and append the page to EXER8A.
6. Clear the screen without resaving EXER10A.
7. Exit WordPerfect or complete the next exercise.

10B Complete the following tasks:

1. Retrieve EXER8A. Look for the appended text.
2. Delete the [Tab Set] code on the line beginning with "Search." It was appended but is not necessary now.
3. Position the cursor on the [BOLD] or [ITALC] code before "Search." Choose EDIT, SELECT from the menu to move this paragraph. Position the cursor on the [BOLD] or [ITALC] code before "Layout," and retrieve the text.
4. Repeat these steps to arrange the following paragraphs (lines). Be careful about the position of the [BOLD] or [ITALC] codes.

MENU	OPTIONS
File	Retrieve, Print, List Files, Save, Exit
Edit	Undelete, Reveal Codes
Search	Forward, Backward, Go To
Layout	Line, Page
Mark	Index, Define, Generate
Tools	Spell Thesaurus, Date Text
Font	Base Font, Appearance, Size
Graphics	Figure, Equation, Line
Help	Help, Index, Template

5. Save your document as EXER10B. Print a copy.
6. Exit WordPerfect or go on to the next topic.

1 page

Aligning Text

CONCEPTS Horizontal centering is used to emphasize. It sets text apart from lines that start at the left margin. Vertical centering positions text so that it is centered from the top to the bottom of the page. There is an equal amount of white space above and below the lines. If you were preparing an advertising bulletin or a flyer, your text might be more prominent if it were horizonally and vertically centered. Other special alignment features include justification options for how the margins appear.

Centering Text Horizontally 90

A Center command positions the text between the left and the right margins so that an equal amount of white space is on either side of the text. In WordPerfect, you give the Center command and then type the text. The software moves the cursor to the center point of your page and backs up one time for every two characters that you type. When you press ENTER to complete the line, the Center command is canceled. To type another centered line, you need to give the Center command again.

With most Center commands, you can insert or delete words on the line. The text is automatically recentered. If you change the margins, the text is recentered according to the new margins. You can apply the Center command to text that is already typed. You can remove centering by deleting the electronic code that causes the text to be centered. ◄

> **TIP** In WordPerfect, you can use the Block command to center several lines at once. Type everything at the left margin, block it, and apply the Center command.

Centering Text Vertically 90

WordPerfect has top and bottom margins and counts the lines as you type. It can mathematically determine how much top and bottom margin is needed for the text to appear in the middle of the page. WordPerfect does this when you give the command to vertically center the page.

If you add or delete lines from the page, the text is recentered. In WordPerfect, a command to vertically center a page pertains only to that page. When you start a new page, the text resumes its usual top and bottom margins unless you give another Center Page command.

Justifying Text 

Justification refers to the way in which text aligns at the margins. Your software has a default setting for the justification of text. Popular justification settings are left, right, and full. Figure 11.1 displays three types of justification.

Figure 11.1
Left-, Full-, and Right-justified Paragraphs

```
This is a paragraph typed with left justification. The lines are
aligned at the left margin and have a ragged right margin. Such
text is fairly easy to read.

  This paragraph is typed with right justification. The lines are
   aligned at the right margin with a ragged left margin. This is
                         rather difficult to read for most people.

This paragraph illustrates full justification. The margins are even
on the left and the right. The printer, however, will insert or
remove spaces as necessary to even out the lines.
```

TIP: WordPerfect has Center Justification. This alignment horizontally centers each line as you type it so that you do not need to repeat the Center command for each line.

Text that is left justified has an even left margin with a ragged right margin. Such text is easy to read because your eye always returns to the same location for the start of the next line. Right-justified text is aligned at the right margin with a ragged left margin. This type of alignment is used only for special effect. It is difficult to read because your eye has to locate the start of each line. Full justification uses even left and right margins. The printer condenses or expands spaces to fill out the line. Depending on your printer, these spaces may be noticeable. ◀

Right-Aligning Text

91

A Flush Right command can be used to type a single line so that it ends at the right margin. This command may be more efficient than a justification command when only one line is to be right aligned. A typical use of right-aligned text is a date or a signature that appears even with the right margin. A Right-Align command is canceled when you press ENTER.

Like other align features, you can insert or delete text from a line that is flush right. Your software will probably also allow you to insert or delete the flush right alignment, too.

Using Indents

91

An indent is similar to a temporary left margin because the text aligns at a new position. When you press ENTER, the indent is canceled and the regular left margin is resumed. The indent feature uses tab settings to align text. If no tabs are set, the indent feature does not work.

Common uses for this type of alignment are numbered paragraphs or long quotations. As you type the paragraph, wordwrap returns the cursor to the temporary indent position so that the paragraph is aligned as shown in Figure 11.2.

Figure 11.2
Numbered Paragraphs and Quotation

```
     1.   This is an example of an indented paragraph. As you
          type the cursor does not return to the left margin
          until you press Enter. Wordwrap returns the cursor to
          the point where the text is aligned.

We are all somewhat familiar with the speech made by Abraham
Lincoln. Here are the first few lines.

     Fourscore and seven years ago our fathers brought forth
     upon this continent a new nation, conceived in liberty,
     and dedicated to the proposition that all men are created
     equal. Now we are engaged in a great civil war, testing
     whether that nation, or any nation so conceived and so
     dedicated, can long endure.
```

TUTORIAL In this tutorial, you type a document with lines centered horizontally. You type paragraphs with different justification settings and use flush right for individual lines. You also use indent to type a list. Change the current directory if necessary, and insert your document disk in drive A: to save your work.

1 Center text horizontally.

Select	"Layout"	Displays Layout menu.
Select	"Align"	Displays Align menu.
Select	"Center"	Moves cursor to center of line.

The horizontal center of a 8.5 × 11-inch piece of paper is 4.25".

Type	(your first name and your last name)	Centers your name as you type.
Press	↵ ENTER	Cancels centering.

The cursor returns to the left margin. You can execute the Center command from the keyboard with the Shift-F6 key.

Select	"Layout," "Align," "Center"	Moves cursor to center.
Type	(your street address)	Centers your address.
Press	↵ ENTER	Cancels centering.
Select	"Layout," "Align," "Center"	Moves cursor to center.
Type	(your city, state, and ZIP)	Centers line.
Press	↵ ENTER twice	Cancels centering.
Press	PAGE UP	Moves cursor to top of page.
Press	CTRL-→ twice	Moves cursor to first character of last name.
Type	(your middle name)	Inserts your name
Press	SPACEBAR	Inserts a space.

The line is recentered as you type.

Press	↓	Moves cursor to address line.

Watch the screen to determine how many times to press Control-Left or Control-Right to position the cursor anywhere in the street name.

Press	CTRL-← or CTRL-→	Moves cursor to street name.
Press	CTRL-←BACKSPACE	Deletes a word.

The line is recentered after you delete text.

Select	"Edit," "Undelete," "Restore"	Restores street name.
Press	PAGE UP	Moves cursor to top of document.
Press	F11	Displays [Center] code.
Press	DELETE	Deletes [Center] code.

The text starts at the left margin.

Select	"Layout," "Align," "Center"	Inserts [Center] code.

2 **Center page vertically.** Your name and address should be on the screen with the codes revealed.

Press	HOME three times, ↑	Moves cursor to top of page.
Select	"Layout," "Page"	Displays Page Format menu.
Select	"Center Page (top to bottom)"	Moves cursor to option.
Select	"Yes"	Enters center page setting.
Press	F7	Inserts [Center Pg] code.

The [CenterPg] code must be the first code on the page. There should be no text, not even a space, before it. The Center Page command is canceled when you start a new page. You can execute the Center Page command from the keyboard with the Shift-F8 key.

Select	"File," "Print," "View Document"	Displays View screen.

Vertical centering is visible in the view screen.

Press	F7	Returns to document.
Press	←BACKSPACE	Deletes [Center Pg] code.
Select	"File," "Print," "View Document"	Document has default top margin.
Press	F7	Returns to document.

3 **Justify text.** Your name and address should be on the screen with the codes revealed.

Press	PAGE DOWN	Moves cursor to bottom of page.
Select	"Layout," "Justify"	Displays Justify menu.

There are four justification choices.

Select	"Left"	Inserts a [Just:Left] code.

Type the following paragraph. The text aligns at the left margin.

```
    The Move command in WordPerfect allows you to rearrange
your text without having to retype it. Move is a combination
of the Delete and Insert commands. Text is deleted from its
original location and inserted into the new location.
```

Press	↵ENTER twice	Ends paragraph.

You can execute the Justification command from the keyboard with the Shift-F8 key.

Select	"Layout," "Justify," "Right"	Inserts a [Just:Right] code.

The cursor moves to the right margin. The text aligns at the right margin as you type. Type the following paragraph.

```
  The Copy command allows you to quickly repeat a portion of the
 text on the same page, a different page, or even in a different
        document. WordPerfect will leave the text in the original
                   location and duplicate it in the new location.
```

Press	↵ENTER twice	Ends paragraph.

A justification setting remains in effect until you enter a new justification code.

Select	"Layout," "Justify," "Full"	Inserts a [Just:Full] code.

Type the following paragraph. Right Justification is not visible on the document edit screen.

```
    The Append command will place a copy of the text at the
end of a different document. That document does not have to
be retrieved in order to add to it. As a matter of fact,
WordPerfect will create a new document for you and add the
text to the newly created document.
```

Press	↵ENTER twice	Ends paragraph.
Select	"File," "Save"	Displays Save prompt.
Type	topic11	Enters filename.
Press	↵ENTER	Saves TOPIC11.
Select	"File," "Print," "Page"	Prints page.

TIP The Flush Right command produces the same results as Right Justification. Flush Right is in effect for only one line. The command must be given at the beginning of every line.

4 Flush right text. TOPIC11 is on the screen with the codes revealed.

Press	PAGE DOWN	Moves cursor to bottom of page.
Select	"Layout," "Align," "Flush Right"	Inserts a [Flsh Rgt] code.

The cursor moves to the right margin. ◀

Type	Sincerely,	Aligns text at right margin.
Press	↵ENTER four times	Cancels Flush Right.

You can execute the Flush Right command from the keyboard with the ALT-F6 key.

Select	"Layout," "Align," "Flush Right"	Inserts a [Flsh Rgt] code.
Type	(your first name and your last name)	Aligns text at right margin.
Press	↵ENTER twice	Cancels Flush Right.
Press	F11	Removes Codes screen.

5 Using indent.

Select	"Layout," "Line," "Tab Set"	Displays tab ruler.
Press	CTRL-END	Deletes all tabs.
Type	0.5	Enters new tab setting.
Press	↵ENTER	Enters "L" at +0.5".
Type	1	Enters new tab setting.
Press	↵ENTER	Enters "L" at +1".
Press	F7 twice	Returns to document.

You can click on the right mouse button to return to the document from the tab ruler line.

Press	F11	Displays [Tab Set] code.
Type	1.	Enters "1." at left margin.
Select	"Layout," "Align," "Indent ->"	Inserts [→ Indent] code.

The cursor moves to the first tab setting. Type the following question.

```
How do you save a document that has already been saved using
a different name?
```

Press	↵ ENTER twice	Cancels indent.

You can execute the Indent command from the keyboard with the F4 key.

Press	TAB	Moves cursor to first tab setting.
Type	a)	Enters "a)" at first tab.
Select	"Layout," "Align," "Indent -> <-"	Inserts [→Indent←] code.

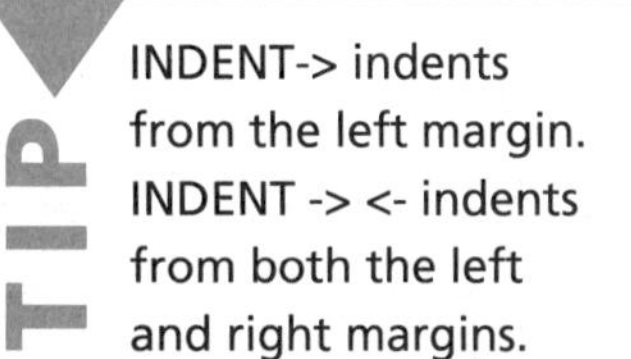

The cursor moves to the next tab setting.
Type the following sentence.

```
Press F10 and then press the ESC key to remove the existing
filename.
```

Press	↵ ENTER twice	Cancels indent.

You can execute the Indent -> <- command from the keyboard with the Shift-F4 Key.

Press	TAB	Moves cursor to first tab setting.
Type	b)	Enters "b)" at first tab.
Select	"Layout," "Align," "Indent -> <-"	Inserts [→Indent←] code.

Type the following sentence.

```
Press F5 and ENTER to accept the default directory; then
highlight the filename and select RENAME/MOVE.
```

Press	↵ ENTER twice	Cancels indent.

Repeat the steps to add the next option.

```
c)   Start the Save command and type the new name over the
     existing name.
```

Press	↵ENTER twice	Cancels indent.
Press	F11	Removes Codes screen.
Select	"File," "Save"	Displays Save prompt.
Press	↵ENTER	Enters filename.
Select	Y	Resaves TOPIC11.
Select	"File," "Print," "Page"	Prints page.
Select	"File," "Exit," "No," "No"	Clears screen.

PROCEDURE SUMMARY

CENTERING TEXT HORIZONTALLY

Activate the menu bar.	ALT-=
Select "Layout," "Align," "Center."	L, A, C
Type the text.	(your input)
End Center.	↵ENTER

CENTERING TEXT VERTICALLY

Position the cursor at the beginning of the page before all codes.	HOME, HOME, HOME, ↑
Activate the menu bar.	ALT-=
Select "Layout," "Page."	L, P
Select "Center Page (top to bottom)."	C or 1
Select "Yes."	Y

JUSTIFYING TEXT

Position the cursor where justification should be changed or started.	
Activate the menu bar.	ALT-=
Select "Layout," "Line."	L, L
Select "Justification."	J or 3

Select "Left," "Right," "Center," or "Full."	L or R or C or F
Accept the new justification.	F7

RIGHT-ALIGNING TEXT

Activate the menu bar.	ALT-=
Select "Layout," "Align," "Flush Right."	L, A, F
Type the text.	(your input)
End Flush Right.	↵ ENTER

USING INDENT

Activate the menu bar.	ALT-=
Select "Layout," "Align," "Indent ->" or "Indent-> <-."	L, A, I, or N
Type the text.	(your input)
End Indent.	↵ ENTER

EXERCISES

11A Complete the following tasks:

1. Type the document shown here. Center the title and use the Very Large font size. Move the cursor past the [vry large] code. Press ENTER twice after the title.
2. Set two tabs at +0.5" and +1".
3. Change to double spacing before the first paragraph.
4. Type the first paragraph. Press ENTER once after it.
5. Change to single spacing before the first numbered paragraph.
6. Press TAB to indent the number. Type the number and the period. Then use Indent-> <- to indent the numbered paragraphs from both margins. Press ENTER twice at the end of each paragraph.

WAYS TO REDUCE STRESS

As a student, an employee, and a family member, you are subject to many stressful situations. Learn to take things in stride by observing a few simple principles.

1. Be sure to get enough sleep each night. If necessary, set an alarm clock to remind yourself when it is time to go to bed.

2. Do not worry about the flustering daily occurrences. Think of your next embarrassing moment as an episode on The Country's Funniest Videos.

3. Instead of doing something tomorrow, do it today. Instead of doing something later today, do it now. Hard work is simply the things you did not do when you should have.

Do not forget the importance of a well-balanced diet and exercise, too. By combining these ideas, you can learn to savor each moment.

7. Press ENTER twice after the third numbered paragraph. Change to double spacing. Type the last paragraph.
8. Save your document as EXER11A. Print a copy.
9. Exit WordPerfect or complete the next exercise.

11B Complete the following tasks:

1. Retrieve EXER9B.
2. Position the cursor at the top of the page before any codes. Reveal the codes.
3. Enter the [Center Pg] code.
4. As the second code on the page, change your default Justification setting. If you normally use Full Justification, change to Left. If you regularly use Left Justification, change to Full. Remove the Codes screen.
5. Position the cursor at the bottom of the page. Press ENTER one time to position the cursor on a line by itself at the left margin. Use Flush Right to type the current date at the right margin. Press ENTER one time after the date.
6. View the document and then print it.
7. Resave EXER9B.
8. Exit WordPerfect or go on to the next topic.

Searching and Replacing

CONCEPTS If you need to verify information or check the spelling of someone's name, you can use Search to quickly find the word. You can combine Search with Replace to make multiple revisions to a document without retyping. If you typed a letter in which you referred to the wrong person four times, you can use Replace to locate and change the name.

Searching for Text or Codes

98

A Search command is usually started at the beginning of a document and proceeds through the document until it finds the first occurrence of your search string, which is the word(s) and codes that you type. When the first string is found, the cursor stops. You then can insert another word, change the word, delete it, and so on. Most software allows you to continue searching for the same string by starting the Search command again. The search resumes from the current cursor position and moves forward until the next occurrence is found.

When you search for text, you need to type enough of the word or phrase to distinguish it from other words. To look for the word "theater," you need to type more than "the." A search string of "the" would find every occurrence of the word "the," "these," "theme," and so on in addition to "theater."

If you want to find instances of a complete word such as "up," include the space after the word as part of the search string. Otherwise, the Search command finds all occurrences of "up" whether they are at the beginning, in the middle, or the end of a word, as in "upon," "upper," "supper," "backup."

Searches may be case sensitive, depending on the software. In WordPerfect, a string typed in lowercase letters finds all occurrences of the word whether they are upper or lowercase. A string typed in uppercase letters finds only the uppercase versions of the word.

WordPerfect allows you to search backward through the document. This is helpful if you have just finished typing and the cursor is at the end of the document.

TIP Since a Replace command can make many changes to a document, you should save the document with a different name before or after doing the replace. In this way, you keep a copy of the original document.

Searching and Replacing Text

99

A Replace command combines Search with Delete/Insert. Before the search is carried out, you type a replacement string. This is the text or codes that will replace the text or codes that the search locates. When the word or code is found, it is automatically replaced with whatever you typed. ◀

Replacing starts at the current cursor position. If you do a forward replace beginning on page 3, pages 1 and 2 are ignored. WordPerfect is able to replace forward and backward through the document.

A common feature of a Replace command is to replace each occurrence individually or globally. Individual replacement means that you can see the substitution on the screen and indicate yes or no. A global replacement means that the software goes through the document and replaces every occurrence without your involvement.

The search part of a Replace command has the same case sensitivity as a regular Search command. You can type the search string in lowercase letters to find all instances or in uppercase letters to find only the uppercase versions. The Replace string, however, is case sensitive. Whatever you type as a replacement is what will be inserted into your document. If you want the replacement to be all caps, you need to type all caps. If you want initial caps only, that is what you need to type.

TUTORIAL

In this tutorial, you search for and replace text and codes. Change the current directory if necessary, and insert your document disk in drive A: to save your work.

1 Search for text.

Select	"File," "Retrieve"	Displays Retrieve prompt.
Type	exer11a	Enters filename.
Press	↵ENTER	Retrieves EXER11A.
Select	"Search"	Displays Search menu.

The Search menu (see Figure 12.1) includes options for the search direction, for repeating the search, and for choosing the Replace or the Go To command.

Select	"Forward"	Displays "-> Srch:".
Type	you	Enters search string.

Do not press Enter to continue a search activity. If you press Enter, you insert an [HRt] code as part of the search string. Press Backspace to delete it.

Press	F2	Moves cursor to space after "you."

A search moves the cursor one character to the right of the search string. The cursor is at the space between "you" and "are." You can execute the Forward Search command from the keyboard with the F2 key.

Figure 12.1
Search Menu

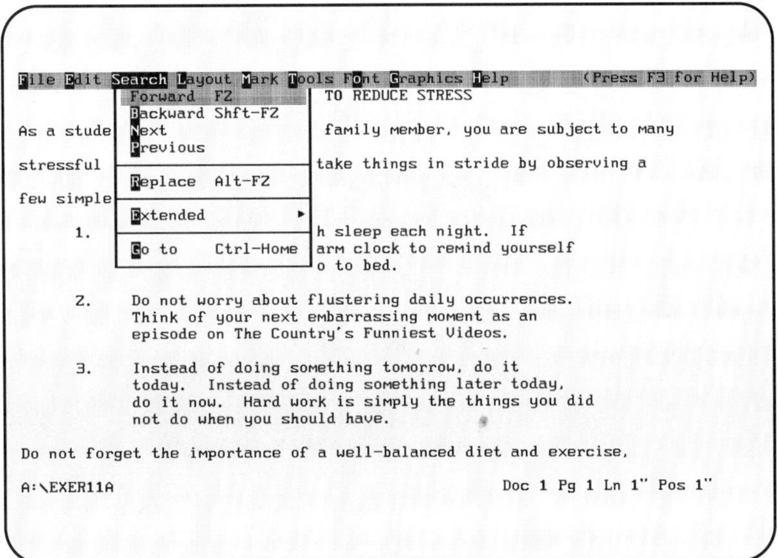

Select	"Search," "Next"	Moves cursor to next occurrence.

The next occurrence of "you" is in "yourself."

Select	"Search," "Next"	Moves cursor to "r" in "your".
Select	"Search," "Next"	Moves cursor to space between "you" and "did".
Select	"Search," "Next"	Moves cursor to space between "you" and "should".
Select	"Search," "Next"	Moves cursor to space between "you" and "can".
Select	"Search," "Next"	Displays "* Not found *".

The cursor does not move. Your system may beep after some activities, such as an ended search.

Select	"Search," "Backward"	Displays "<- Srch: you".

Your most recent search string appears at the "<- Srch:" prompt. It is removed when you type a new string.

Type	it	Enters new search string.
Press	F2	Moves cursor between "it" and "now".

You can execute the Backward Search command from the keyboard with the Shift-F2 key.

> **TIP** Add a space to a search string (it) so that words like "situations" are not found. When you use this method, a search does not find "it" followed by a punctuation mark.

Select	"Search," "Previous"	Moves cursor between "it" and "today."
Select	"Search," "Previous"	Moves cursor between "it" and "is."
Select	"Search," "Previous"	Moves cursor to next occurrence.

The next occurrence of "it" is in "situations." ◀

2 Search for codes.

Select	"Search," "Forward"	Displays "-> Srch: it".

Your most recent search string is displayed.

> **TIP** You can return the cursor to its original position after a search by pressing CTRL-HOME twice.

Press	TAB	Enters [Tab] as search string.
Press	F2	Moves cursor to "1" after [Tab] code.
Select	"Search," "Next"	Moves cursor to "2".
Select	"Search," "Next"	Moves cursor to "3".
Press	PAGE DOWN	Moves cursor to bottom of page.
Select	"Search," "Backward"	Displays "<- Srch: [Tab]".

The arrow in the message line shows the search direction. ◀

Press	↵ ENTER	Enters [HRt] as search string.
Press	F2	Moves cursor to "D" in "Do".

The [HRt] code is on the previous line.

Select	"Search," "Previous"	Moves cursor to [HRt] code.
Select	"File," "Exit," "No," "No"	Clears screen.

3 Replace text.

Select	"File," "Retrieve"	Displays Retrieve prompt.
Type	exer9a	Enters filename.
Press	↵ ENTER	Retrieves EXER9A.
Select	"Search," "Replace"	Displays "w/Confirm?"

No confirmation means that replacements are made automatically.

Select	"No"	Displays "-> Srch: [HRt]".
Type	disk	Enters new search string.
Press	F2	Displays "Replace with:"
Type	diskette	Enters replacement string.

The search string is the text that will be found. The replacement string will be substituted at each occurrence of the search string.

Press	F2	Makes replacements.

The cursor is positioned on the last replacement. You can execute the Replace command from the keyboard with the Alt-F2 key.

Press	PAGE UP	Moves cursor to top of page.

TIP You can use Replace to speed up your typing. If your document refers to "Boyd & Fraser Publishing Company" several times, you could initially type "BF." When you finish typing the document, replace "BF" with the full name. The maximum length of a search string is 59 characters or codes.

"Disk" was replaced with "Diskette" in the title, and "disks" was replaced with "diskettes" in the second paragraph.

Press	PAGE DOWN	Moves cursor to bottom of page.
Select	"Search," "Replace"	Displays "with Confirm?"
Select	"No"	Displays "-> Srch: disk".
Type	diskette	Enters search string.
Press	↑	Changes search direction.

The prompt is "<- Srch: diskette" to show a backward search/replace. There is no menu or keyboard command for Backward Replace. Use the Up Arrow to change the direction. ◀

Press	F2	Displays "Replace with:"
Type	disk	Enters replacement string.
Press	F2	Makes replacements.

4 Replace codes.

Select	"Search," "Replace"	Displays "with Confirm?"
Select	"Yes"	Displays Search prompt.
Press	TAB	Enters code as search string.
Press	F2	Displays "Replace with:"

Press	TAB twice	Enters two codes as replacement string.
Press	F2	Moves cursor to first [Tab].

The replacement is not made. The prompt is "Confirm? No (Yes)."

Select	"Yes"	Replaces one tab with two.

The cursor moves to the next [Tab]. The prompt is "Confirm? No (Yes)."

Select	"Yes"	Makes replacement.

Make the same replacement for the last paragraph.

Press	PAGE UP	Moves cursor to top of page.

All the paragraphs have two tabs now. ◀

TIP When responding to a "-> Srch:" prompt, you cannot use the menu bar to enter codes for a tab, a hard return, an indent, line spacing, flush right, and so on. You must use the keyboard command.

Select	"Search," "Replace"	Displays "with Confirm?"
Select	"Yes"	Displays "-> Srch: [Tab]".
Press	TAB twice	Enters new search string.
Press	F2	Displays "Replace with:"
Press	TAB	Enters replacement string.
Press	F2	Moves cursor to [Tab] [Tab].

The replacement is not made. The prompt is "Confirm? No (Yes)."

Select	"Yes"	Replaces two tabs with one.

The cursor moves to the next [Tab] [Tab]. The prompt is "Confirm? No (Yes)." Make the replacements for the other two paragraphs. ◀

Select	"File," "Exit," "No," "No"	Clears screen.

TIP You can use the Replace command as a Search and Delete command. For example, delete underline codes by searching for [UND] and replacing it with nothing. In response to the "Replace with" prompt, just press F2.

PROCEDURE SUMMARY

SEARCHING FOR TEXT OR CODES

Activate the menu bar.	ALT - =
Select "Search."	S
Select the search direction.	F or B

Enter the search string.	(your input)
Perform the search.	F2

SEARCHING AND REPLACING TEXT

Activate the menu bar.	ALT-=
Select "Search."	S
Select "Replace."	R
Respond to the "w/Confirm?" prompt.	Y or N
Enter the search string.	(your input)
Accept the search string.	F2
Enter the replacement string.	(your input)
Perform the replace.	F2
Respond to the "Confirm?" prompt if necessary.	Y or N

EXERCISES

12A Complete the following tasks:

1. Retrieve EXER10B.
2. Position the cursor at the top of the page to search for [BOLD] or [ITALC] codes. If you used bold in your document, press F6 to enter the [BOLD] code in response to the "-> Srch:" prompt. If you used italic, press Control-F8 and select Appearance, Italc to insert the [ITALC] code. Press F2 to perform the search.
3. Select Search, Next to find the next occurrence. Repeat this a few times.
4. Return the cursor to the top of the page.
5. Start the Replace command. In response to the "w/Confirm?" prompt, select No.
6. If you used bold in your document, press F6 to enter the [BOLD] code in response to the "-> Srch:" prompt. If you used italic, press Control-F8 and select Appearance, Italc to insert the [ITALC] code. Press F2 to continue.
7. In response to the "Replace with" prompt, press F2. The [BOLD] or [ITALC] codes are removed because they are replaced with nothing.

8. View your document and print it.
9. Clear the screen without resaving EXER10B.
10. Exit WordPerfect or complete the next exercise.

12B Complete the following tasks:

1. Type the following document. Set one tab at the center of the page, +3.25".

```
                                    Today's Date

Your Title, First Name, Last Name
Your Street Address
Your City, State, ZIP

Dear Your First Name:

Thank you for opening your checking account at First
National Bank. I would also like to suggest that we act as
your Federal Tax Depository.

A booklet about services at First National Bank is enclosed
for your review. It should answer all your questions about
the numerous benefits we offer.

We want you to be happy that you bank with First National
Bank. Please call me if you have any concerns.

                                    Sincerely yours,



                                    Audrey Long
                                    Customer Services

Enclosure

xx/exer12b
```

2. Save the document as EXER12B. Print a copy and leave the document on the screen.
3. Position the cursor at the top of the page. Start the Replace command.
4. In response to the "w/Confirm?" prompt, select No.
5. In response to the "-> Srch:" prompt, type "First National." Do not leave a space after "National." If you do, the search will try to find and replace the word and the space after it. You need the space for the inserted word. Press F2.
6. In response to the "Replace with" prompt, type "United Savings." Do not space after "Savings." If you do, you will insert an extra space with the word because the space is already before "Bank." Press F2.
7. Save the new document as EXER12B2. Print a copy.
8. Exit WordPerfect or go on to the next topic.

Using Spell and the Thesaurus

TIP

A utility is a software program separate from the main program. It works with the main program to accomplish a task. Examples of utility programs are spellers, thesauruses, and conversion.

CONCEPTS On a computer screen, it is easy to miss typographical errors. The lighting, the screen colors, the uniform size of characters, and screen scrolling all contribute to a situation in which your eye has to work harder than normal. A spelling utility can find many errors for you. If you are writing an important letter or a class report, you probably do not want to use the same word(s) too often. An electronic thesaurus, another utility, finds words with the same meaning so that your writing has some variety.

Checking Spelling

107

A spell program is an electronic dictionary. WordPerfect has over 100,000 words in the dictionary. That is a large amount, but certainly not all the words in the language. A word may be marked as misspelled even though it is correct; it is just not in the electronic list.

When you spell check a document, words on the screen are matched against words in the dictionary. If no match is found, the word is flagged as misspelled. Proper names such as large cities and states might be included in the list, but generally proper names are not in the electronic dictionary. Other words that might not be in the dictionary are terms used in specialized industries or professions, popular abbreviations, and acronyms.

A spell program locates misspelled words and offers choices for the correct spelling on the screen. Alternative spellings are found based on the characters in the misspelled word. If you type "teh," the program finds words with similar letters and allows you to choose the correct spelling. The alternatives might be "tea," "the," "ten," "tee," and others.

WordPerfect allows you to check a page, the entire document, a block of text, or just a word. In most cases, you will want to check the entire document. You may be able to "look up" a word, too, using wildcard characters (* and ?) like a DOS command. Many spell programs check for double words and irregular capitalization, too.

The speller lessens your proofreading time, but it does not eliminate it. It does not find all errors. If you type "their," but the word should be "there," a speller does not mark it as a misspelled word. "Their" is a properly spelled word; it is just grammatically wrong.

You can add words to the electronic dictionary if you have your own software. You can add names or abbreviations that you use often so that they are not found as misspelled every time you spell check your work.

Using the Thesaurus (107)

A thesaurus is a list of words with similar meanings. When you use an electronic thesaurus, you first select a word to be investigated. The software finds the word and displays other words with the same meaning. WordPerfect lists words with opposite meanings.

Sometimes the list of replacement words does not contain what you want. You might be able to choose one of the words in the list and look it up to investigate further.

When you select a replacement word, make sure that it is the correct form. Like the spell utility, the thesaurus does not always make the correct grammatical choice.

TUTORIAL In this tutorial, you retrieve a document and insert deliberate errors. Then you use Spell to find the errors and make the corrections. You also use the Thesaurus to find replacements for several words. Change the current directory if necessary, and insert your document disk in drive A: to save your work.

1 **Check the spelling.** Edit EXER12B to insert deliberate spelling errors.

Select	"File," "Retrieve"	Displays Retrieve prompt.
Type	exer12b	Enters filename.
Press	↵ ENTER	Retrieves EXER12B.
Select	"Search," "Forward"	Displays "-> Srch:".

Your most recent search string may be displayed.

Type	acc	Enters search string.
Press	F2	Moves cursor to "account."
Press	← BACKSPACE	Deletes second "c."
Select	"Search," "Forward"	Displays "-> Srch: acc".
Type	to	Enters search string.
Press	SPACEBAR	Adds a space to search string.
Press	F2	Moves cursor to space after "to".
Press	DELETE	Deletes "s" in "suggest".
Select	"Search," "Forward"	Displays "-> Srch: to".
Type	is	Enters search string.
Press	SPACEBAR	Adds a space to search string.

Press	F2	Moves cursor to space after "is".
Press	DELETE	Deletes "e" in "enclosed".
Type	i	Changes word to "inclosed".
Select	"Search," "Forward"	Displays "-> Srch: is".
Type	rev	Enters search string.

You can search for the word "review" without typing the entire word.

Press	F2	Moves cursor to "rev".
Press	DELETE	Deletes "i" in "review."
Press	→	Moves cursor to "w" in "revew."
Type	i	Changes word to "reveiw."
Select	"Search," "Forward"	Displays "-> Srch: rev".
Type	want	Enters search string.
Press	F2	Moves cursor to "want".
Press	SPACEBAR	Inserts a space.
Type	want	Inserts word.

The sentence reads "We want want you to be happy . . ."

Select	"Search," "Forward"	Displays "-> Srch: want".
Type	Pl	Enters "Pl" as search string.
Press	F2	Moves cursor to "Please".
Press	←BACKSPACE	Deletes "l" in "Please".
Type	L	Changes word to "PLease".
Select	"Tools"	Displays Tools menu.
Select	"Spell"	Displays Spell menu.
Select	"Document"	Starts spell-check.

The first misspelled word, a proper name in the address, is highlighted. Skip a proper name that is spelled correctly.

Select	"2 Skip"	Moves cursor to next misspelled word.
Select	"2 Skip"	Moves cursor to next misspelled word.

Skip all proper names in the address until "acount" is highlighted and a list of alternatives is displayed as shown in Figure 13.1. If you have errors of your own, they will also be found as misspelled.

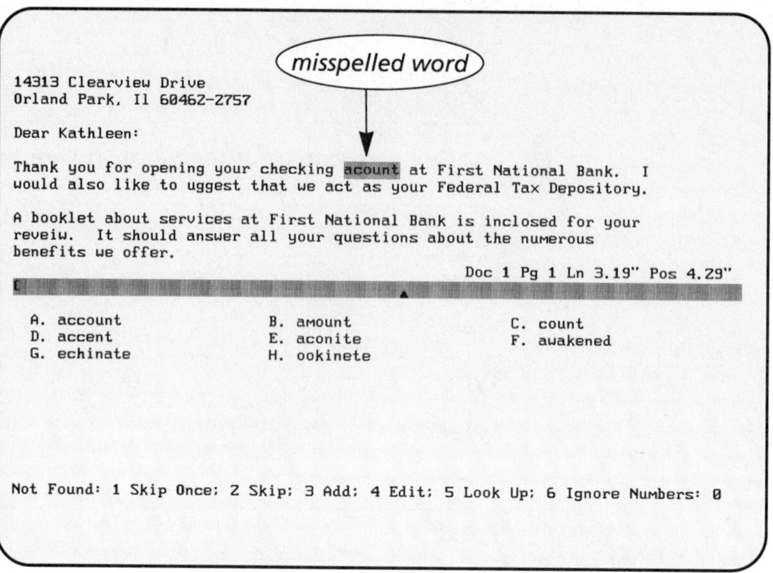

misspelled word
14313 Clearview Drive
Orland Park, Il 60462-2757
Dear Kathleen:
Thank you for opening your checking acount at First National Bank. I would also like to uggest that we act as your Federal Tax Depository.
A booklet about services at First National Bank is inclosed for your reveiw. It should answer all your questions about the numerous benefits we offer.
Doc 1 Pg 1 Ln 3.19" Pos 4.29"
A. account
B. amount
C. count
D. accent
E. aconite
F. awakened
G. echinate
H. ookinete
Not Found: 1 Skip Once; 2 Skip; 3 Add; 4 Edit; 5 Look Up; 6 Ignore Numbers: 0

Figure 13.1
EXER12B with "acount" Shown as Error

Press	A	Chooses option A.

The correction is made when you type the letter. Spell-checking continues, and the next word is highlighted. There is no alternative spelling for "uggest."

Select	"4 Edit"	Moves cursor to "uggest".
Type	s	Inserts "s".
Press	F7	Resumes spell-checking.

The next misspelled word should be "reveiw."

Press	A	Makes correction.

The next error is "want want." The prompt is "Double Word."

Select	"3 Delete 2nd"	Deletes second word.

The next error is "PLease." The prompt is "Irregular Case."

Select	"3 Replace"	Replaces "L".

The next error should be shown as "Audrey," a proper name.

Select	"2 Skip"	Skips word.

The next error is the document name.

Select	"2 Skip"	Skips word.

The word count is shown, and the prompt is "Press any key to continue."

Press	SPACEBAR	Ends Spell.

You can execute the Spell command from the keyboard with the Control-F2 key.

Select	"Search," "Backward"	Displays "<- Srch:".
Type	inclos	Enters search string.
Press	F2	Moves cursor to "inclosed".

WordPerfect did not identify "inclosed" as misspelled because it is in the dictionary.

Press	CTRL-←	Moves cursor to "i".
Press	DELETE	Deletes "i".
Type	e	Changes word to "enclosed".

2 Using the thesaurus.

Select	"Search," "Backward"	Displays Search prompt.
Type	sug	Enters search string.
Press	F2	Moves cursor to "suggest".
Select	"Tools," "Thesaurus"	Displays synonyms.

The words are grouped as nouns, adjectives, verbs, or antonyms. Words marked with a bullet (small dot) have their own synonyms.

Select	"Replace Word"	Displays "Press letter for word".
Type	i	Substitutes "recommend".
Select	"Search," "Forward"	Displays Search prompt.
Type	num	Enters search string.
Press	F2	Moves cursor to "numerous".

Select	"Tools," "Thesaurus"	Displays synonyms.
Type	c	Displays synonyms for "many."

The new list appears in the second column with the alphabet selection letters.

Select	"Replace Word"	Displays "Press letter for word".
Type	f	Substitutes "various".
Select	"Search," "Forward"	Displays Search prompt.
Type	hap	Enters search string.
Press	F2	Moves cursor to "happy".
Select	"Tools," "Thesaurus"	Displays synonyms.
Type	c	Displays synonyms for "delighted."

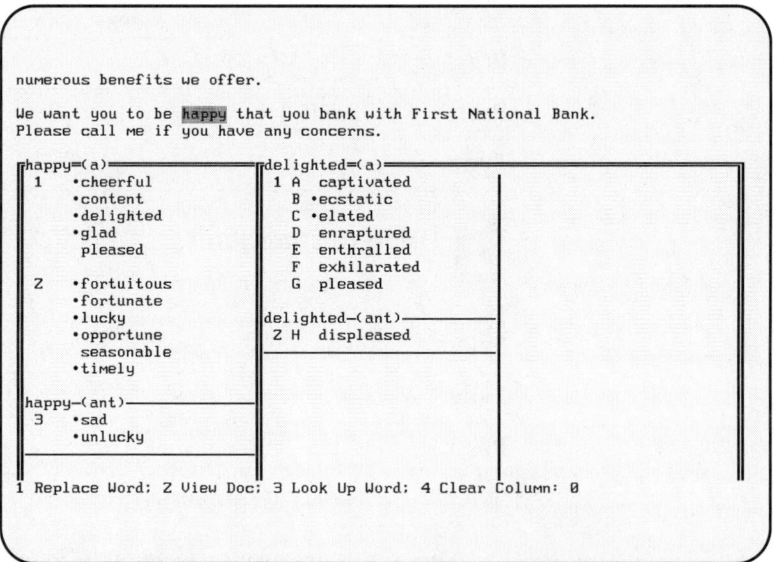

Figure 13.2
Thesaurus with "happy" and "delighted"

Press	←	Moves selection letters.
Select	"Replace Word"	Displays "Press letter for word".
Type	e	Substitutes "pleased".
Select	"File," "Exit," "No," "No"	Clears screen.

You can execute the Thesaurus command from the keyboard with the Alternate-F1 key.

PROCEDURE SUMMARY

CHECKING SPELLING

Activate the menu bar.	ALT - =
Select "Tools."	T
Select "Spell."	E
Select the amount to be checked.	W, P, or D
Select the spell option.	2 or 4
End Spell.	SPACEBAR

USING THE THESAURUS

Position the cursor at the word to be changed.	
Start the Thesaurus command.	
Activate the menu bar.	ALT - =
Select "Tools."	T
Select "Thesaurus."	H
Look up another word if desired.	(your input)
Select "Replace Word."	1
Type the letter of the new word.	(your input)

EXERCISES

13A **Complete the following tasks:**

1. Type the following document. There are deliberate errors in this document.

SAFETY AND COMFORT

The best in technology has resulted in one of the safest yet most comfortable cars on the market today. The new Altonia protects and shelters the driver and passengers.

Driver and passenger air bags. This is an intrecate yet dependible system for emergency restraint.

Flexable steering column. In normal traffic, the column is steady. In case of front impact, the column is designed to give way to limit injury.

Inferior controls. All are designed and shaped for easy accessbility and reduced chance of injury.

Breakaway rearview mirror. The mirror is designed to break away from the windsheild if hit with moderate force.

For more information call 1-800-900-1111 or visit your nearest dealer. Isn't it time you traded up to Altonia?

2. Set tabs at +0.5" and +1" inch. If your default tabs include those settings, you do not need to make any changes.
3. Center the title and use a very large font size. End the font size after the title. Double space after the title.
4. Use bold or italic for the lead-in sentence in the indented paragraphs.
5. Use Indent -> <- for the paragraphs about the features.
6. Use Spell to find and correct planted spelling errors as well as your own errors.
7. Change the word "inferior" to "interior." This was not found as misspelled. It is correctly spelled but is the wrong word.
8. Save your document as EXER13A. Print a copy.

13B Complete the following tasks:

1. Retrieve EXER11A.
2. Use the Thesaurus to find a replacement for "principles" in the first paragraph.
3. Find a replacement word for "flustering" in the second paragraph.
4. Find a replacement word for "savor" in the last paragraph.
5. Resave the document as EXER11A.

Managing Files

CONCEPTS File management is an important part of working with all application software. Deleting files from your disk makes room for new work. You can share files you have created with your friends by making copies. You can change the name of a file if you spelled it incorrectly when you saved the document. If you have to use someone else's disk, you can locate a file if you know how to use a Find command.

> **TIP** Files that have been deleted can be restored with certain DOS recovery programs and the latest versions of DOS.

Deleting a File

113

You should periodically check your disk to see which files can be removed. If you have saved each new revision of a report with a new name, you can probably delete the original versions. It is possible to have files that were created in error, such as saving a blank screen as a file. A filename appears in the list, but when you retrieve it, there is nothing there. Most systems operate most quickly when inactive files are deleted.

When you delete a file from the disk, the files list is updated and the deleted file is no longer listed. Most programs warn you when you delete a file so that you can verify your intentions or change your mind. ◄

Depending on your software, you can delete files one at a time or several at once. To delete several files, you need to mark the files and then give the Delete command.

Copying a File

113

> **TIP** A backup utility program makes a compressed copy of a file. To use a compressed backup file, it needs to be restored to its original state using the same program.

A file can be copied so that you have an identical file on another disk or in a different directory. When you copy a single file, you can use the same filename if the copy is made to another disk. You can make a copy using a different name if you are making the copy on the same disk.

A Copy command requires that you select the file to be copied and indicate where the copy should be made. Usually a Copy command assumes the same filename, but you can specify a different name. If you want to keep two copies of an important report on the same disk, use the Copy command with a different name. You could name them REPORT.ORG and REPORT.BAK so that one is the original and one is a backup.

For important documents, it may be necessary to keep a copy in a different location to guard against loss. Tax records, sales records, or payroll reports are examples of documents that are often kept in duplicate. ◄

Renaming a File

113

When you rename a file, the old name is replaced by the new name. The list of files is updated, and you could then use the old name for another document.

Finding a File

114

A Find command is a search command for the files list. It can look at the filenames or the contents of the files. To look at the filenames, you need to know part or all of the name. WordPerfect also looks at the contents of the files, giving you considerably more capability. If you know that you need the report about nuclear energy but cannot remember the filename, you can search for "nuclear energy" even though that phrase is not in the filename.

A Find command might offer ways to limit the search. You can, for example, look at documents created after a certain date.

TUTORIAL

In this tutorial, you rename, copy, and delete files. You use the Find command to locate files in your directory. Change the current directory if necessary, and insert your document disk in drive A:.

1 Rename a file.

Select	"File," "List Files"	Displays directory name.
Press	↵ ENTER	Lists files.
Select	EXER3B	Highlights filename.
Select	"Move/Rename"	Displays "New name: A:EXER3B."

If you type a filename, the file is renamed. If you type a new directory with the filename, the file is moved to the new location and renamed.

Type	practice	Enters new filename.
Press	↵ ENTER	Renames file.

EXER3B is renamed as PRACTICE and realphabetized in the list.

Select	"Move/Rename"	Displays "New name: A:\PRACTICE."
Type	exer3b	Enters new filename.
Press	↵ ENTER	Renames file.

2 Copy a file using a different name.

The List Files screen should be displayed with EXER3B highlighted.

Select	"Copy"	Displays "Copy this file to."
Type	practice	Enters filename.
Press	↵ ENTER	Copies EXER3B to PRACTICE.

3 **Find a file.** The List Files screen should be displayed with any filename highlighted.

Select	"Find"	Displays Find menu.

Figure 14.1
Find Menu

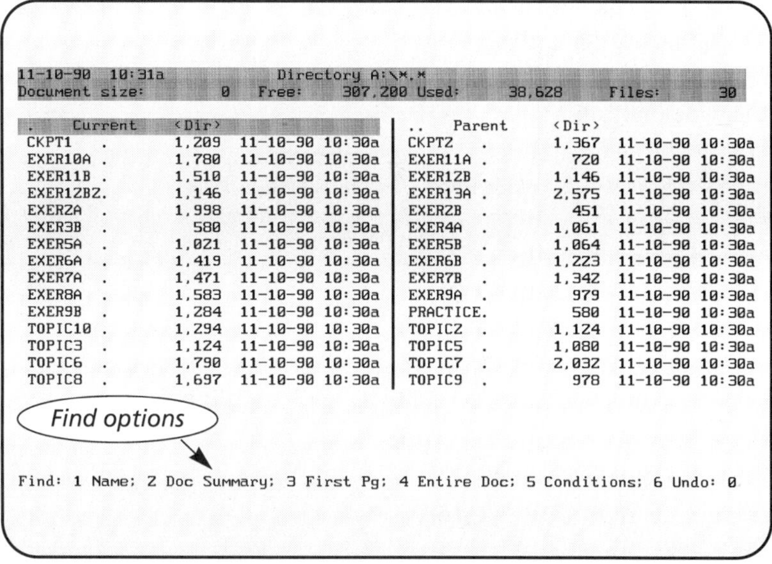

11-10-90 10:31a Directory A:*.*
Document size: 0 Free: 307,200 Used: 38,628 Files: 30
. Current <Dir>
.. Parent <Dir>
CKPT1 . 1,209 11-10-90 10:30a
CKPT2 . 1,367 11-10-90 10:30a
EXER10A . 1,780 11-10-90 10:30a
EXER11A . 720 11-10-90 10:30a
EXER11B . 1,510 11-10-90 10:30a
EXER12B . 1,146 11-10-90 10:30a
EXER12B2. 1,146 11-10-90 10:30a
EXER13A . 2,575 11-10-90 10:30a
EXER2A . 1,998 11-10-90 10:30a
EXER2B . 451 11-10-90 10:30a
EXER3B . 580 11-10-90 10:30a
EXER4A . 1,061 11-10-90 10:30a
EXER5A . 1,021 11-10-90 10:30a
EXER5B . 1,064 11-10-90 10:30a
EXER6A . 1,419 11-10-90 10:30a
EXER6B . 1,223 11-10-90 10:30a
EXER7A . 1,471 11-10-90 10:30a
EXER7B . 1,342 11-10-90 10:30a
EXER8A . 1,583 11-10-90 10:30a
EXER9A . 979 11-10-90 10:30a
EXER9B . 1,284 11-10-90 10:30a
PRACTICE. 580 11-10-90 10:30a
TOPIC10 . 1,294 11-10-90 10:30a
TOPIC2 . 1,124 11-10-90 10:30a
TOPIC3 . 1,124 11-10-90 10:30a
TOPIC5 . 1,080 11-10-90 10:30a
TOPIC6 . 1,790 11-10-90 10:30a
TOPIC7 . 2,032 11-10-90 10:30a
TOPIC8 . 1,697 11-10-90 10:30a
TOPIC9 . 978 11-10-90 10:30a
Find options
Find: 1 Name; 2 Doc Summary; 3 First Pg; 4 Entire Doc; 5 Conditions; 6 Undo: 0

TIP To speed up the Find feature, limit the search to the first page if you know that the word pattern is on the first page.

Select	"Entire Doc"	Displays "Word pattern."

WordPerfect searches the entire contents of each document in your list for the characters that you type.

Type	Altonia	Enters search string.
Press	↵ ENTER	Displays filename with "Altonia."
Select	"Find," "Undo"	Displays full list screen.
Select	"Find," "Entire Doc"	Displays "Word pattern."
Type	Funniest Videos	Enters search string.

Type a Find condition with the appropriate capitalization.

Press	↵ ENTER	Displays filename.

TIP You can print the List Files screen. Display it and give the keyboard print command, Shift-F7.

The highlighted filename contains "Funniest Videos" in the document, not in the name.

Select	"Find"	Displays Find menu.
Select	"Undo"	Displays full list screen.

TIP Name Search is helpful when you have more than a screenload of files. Filenames are in alphabetic order. Typing the initial letter moves the cursor to that portion of the list. Then you may continue typing the filename or use the arrow keys to find a file.

4 **Locate a filename.** The List Files screen should be displayed with any filename highlighted.

Select	"Name Search"	Displays search message.

The List menu is replaced with the "(Name Search; Enter or arrows to Exit)" prompt. ◀

Type	exer11a	Moves highlight to EXER11A.
Press	↵ ENTER	Displays List menu.
Select	"Name Search"	Displays search message.
Type	prac	Moves highlight to PRACTICE.
Press	↵ ENTER	Displays List menu.

5 **Delete files.** The List Files screen should be displayed with "PRACTICE" highlighted.

Select	"Delete"	Displays "Delete A:\PRACTICE?"
Select	"Yes"	Deletes file.
Select	TOPIC2	Highlights filename.
Type	*	Inserts asterisk.

TIP The highlight bar moves from left to right, top to bottom. If you mark a file by mistake, highlight the filename again and type * again to remove the asterisk.

The file is marked with an asterisk before its name. You can mark multiple files for deletion.

Select	EXER2A	Highlights filename.
Type	*	Marks file.
Select	EXER2B	Highlights filename.
Type	*	Marks file.

TIP You can mark all the files at once by pressing [ALT]-[F5]. To unmark all files, press [ALT]-[F5] again. When the files are marked, you can print, delete, rename/move, or copy them.

Highlight and mark other files that you would like to delete, such as files created in error. ◀

Select	"Delete"	Displays "Delete marked files?"
Select	"Yes"	Displays warning. ◀

The prompt is "Marked files will be deleted. Continue?"

Select	"Yes"	Deletes files.
Press	SPACEBAR	Returns to document.

PROCEDURE SUMMARY

DELETING A FILE

Activate the menu bar.	ALT-=
Select "File."	F
Select "List Files."	F
Accept directory.	↵ ENTER
Highlight the filename or mark several files.	(your input) or *
Select the option to delete a file.	D or 2
Respond to the Delete prompt(s).	Y
Remove the List screen.	SPACEBAR

COPYING A FILE

Activate the menu bar.	ALT-=
Select "File."	F
Select "List Files."	F
Accept directory.	↵ ENTER
Highlight the filename.	(your input)
Select the option to copy a file.	C or 8
Type the new filename.	(your input)
Accept the new filename.	↵ ENTER
Remove the List screen.	SPACEBAR

RENAMING A FILE

Activate the menu bar.	ALT-=
Select "File."	F
Select "List Files."	F
Accept directory.	↵ ENTER
Highlight the filename.	(your input)
Select the option to rename a file.	M or 3
Type the new filename.	(your input)
Accept the new filename.	↵ ENTER
Remove the List screen.	SPACEBAR

FINDING A FILE

Activate the menu bar.	ALT-=
Select "File."	F
Select "List Files."	F
Accept directory.	↵ ENTER

To search by word pattern:

Select the option to find a file.	F or 9
Select the amount of text to be searched.	(your input)
Type the word pattern.	(your input)
Accept the word pattern.	↵ ENTER
Remove the filtered List screen.	SPACEBAR

To search by filename:

Select the option to search for a filename.	N
Type the filename.	(your input)
Accept the highlighted filename.	↵ ENTER
Remove the List screen.	SPACEBAR

EXERCISES

14A Complete the following task:

1. List your files to the screen. Use the Find command to find file(s) with the word "stress."
2. Use the Find command to find file(s) with the word "memory."
3. Rename EXER4A as TOPIC4.
4. Copy TOPIC4 to a new file named EXER4A.
5. Remove the list from the screen.

14B Complete the following task:

1. List your files to the screen. Mark the following files with an asterisk:

   EXER3B EXER5B

   EXER4A TOPIC4

   EXER5A
2. Delete these files from your disk.

Checkpoint 2

What You Should Know

- ✓ The appearance of type can be enhanced with bold, underline, italic, and other features if your printer supports these styles. You can also use a different typeface for all or any part of a document.
- ✓ You can block text to identify any portion of a document for use with another command such as delete, save, or print. You can also use the Block command to add styles such as underline and bold to text that is already typed.
- ✓ Text that uses Full justification has even left and right margins. You can also use Right or Left justification as well as Center justification. Justification can be changed several times in a document.
- ✓ The Indent command is a special use of the tab settings that sets a temporary left margin at the tab position. There are two Indent commands, one to indent only from the left margin and one to indent from both margins.
- ✓ A Move command relocates text from one location in a document to another. You can also Copy text so that it appears more than once in a document. An Append command copies text from one document to the end of a second document.
- ✓ The Search command finds text and/or codes in a document. You can search forward or backward through a document. The Replace command finds text and/or codes and replaces the string with a new string.
- ✓ Spell finds misspelled words, double words, and irregular capitalization. A Thesaurus includes synonyms or words with similar meanings. You can look up a word to find a substitute word to add variety to your writing.
- ✓ Files should be deleted from a disk or directory when they are no longer needed. Files can be deleted one at a time or in a batch.

Review Questions

1. What is the command to underline a word as it is typed?
2. How do you change to a different font for the entire document?
3. How can you quickly block a line that ends with a hard return?
4. What prompt appears after you start the Block command?
5. What is the difference between the two Indent commands?
6. When would you use the Flush Right command?
7. What is the difference between Full Justification and Right Justification?
8. What are the differences among Move, Copy, and Append?

9. What is the search string to find upper and lowercase occurrences of the word WORDPERFECT in a document?
10. How can you change the direction of a Replace command?
11. How can you remove all tab codes from a document with one command?
12. What errors are usually not found by the Speller?
13. What is a Thesaurus?
14. How you do mark multiple files in the List Files screen for deletion?

CHECKPOINT PROBLEM A

1. Type the following memo. Set a left tab at +1" and a decimal tab at +4.5".

```
                         MEMORANDUM

TO:         (Your Name)

FROM:       Patricia McMahon

DATE:       Today

SUBJECT:    Price Decreases

I am happy to let you know that we are able to pass along a
decrease in our costs to all customers. Effective the first
of next month, the new prices will be as follows:

      Duplicator Paper                         4.50
      Laser Toner Cartridge                   89.00
      Dot Matrix Ribbons                       7.25
      5 1/4-inch Diskettes                     1.75
      3 1/2-inch Diskettes                     3.50

Please update your sales information to include these
figures.

xx/ckpt2a
```

2. Center the title and use a large font. Triple space after the title.
3. Type the heading words followed by a colon. Press TAB and type the names. To enter the current date, select "Tools," "Date Text." Triple space after the subject line.
4. Type the first paragraph. Press TAB to type each item in the list.
5. Save your work as CKPT2A. Print the memo.
6. Block the phrase "Price Decreases" in the memo heading and add bold or underline.
7. Use the Thesaurus to find a synonym for "happy" in the first paragraph.
8. Resave your work as CKPT2A and print another copy.

CHECKPOINT PROBLEM B

1. The following letter has deliberate errors. Set a left tab at +3.25". This tab is at the center of the page.

```
                          Today's date

Mr. John Marshall
Worldwide Office Products
711 Jorie Boulevard
Dallas, TX 80760-5211

Dear Mr. Marshall:

I would like to express our appreciation for the excellant
customer service your branch has supplied since we instaled
our Aztec Personal Computors. Not only were the computors
instaled efficiently, but the follow-up service has been
outstanding.

We would particularly like to commend Ernesto Marquesa for
his prompt reaction to all our needs. We appreciate his
understanding and consideration in response to the problems
we encountered in the third week of our PC training probram.

The prompt attention from your office has been extremely
important to the progress of our computer applications
training course for the the Dallas County schools.

                          Sincerly yours,



                          Kathleen Stewart, Instructor
                          Office Systems

xx/ckpt2b
```

2. Press ENTER six times to add extra top margin before the date.
3. Press TAB and use the Date feature to enter today's date.
4. Type the paragraphs and closing lines of the letter.
5. Use Spell to correct errors.
6. Save your work as CKPT2B and print a copy.
7. Use the Thesaurus to find alternatives for "reaction" in the second paragraph and "prompt" in the last paragraph.
8. Block the phrase "Aztec Personal Computers" and add bold or underline.
9. Move the second paragraph so that it is the last paragraph in the letter.
10. Resave your work as CKPT2B and print another copy.

Controlling Page Endings

CONCEPTS

Page breaks are necessary for the printer to know when to start a new sheet of paper. A page break is a code that marks the end of one page and the beginning of the next. The process of placing page breaks in a document is sometimes called **pagination**. Most programs today use dynamic pagination because the breaks are inserted as you type. Automatic page breaks can separate a title from its text or split a table. To avoid these situations, WordPerfect allows you to protect your text from being split or to insert your own page breaks.

Using Soft Page Breaks 126

As you type a long document, WordPerfect keeps track of the top and bottom margins and the number of lines. When the page is full, a "soft" page break is inserted to end the page. A **soft page break** is repositioned if you add or delete text on the page. If you delete several paragraphs from a page, text from the next page fills in the space.

Soft page breaks usually cannot be deleted or inserted because they are placed in a document based on the lines you type and on the margins. To display more or less on a page, you can reduce or increase the top or bottom margins. You can also make the left and right margins wider or narrower to squeeze or reduce the amount of text per page.

Keeping Lines Together on a Page 126

You can define a block of text or a certain number of lines to be kept together. If this text falls near the end of a page, WordPerfect moves all the lines to the next page so that the text is not split. You could end up with pages shorter than you intended, but your important information is not split.

Using Widow/Orphan Protection 126

A **widow** is a line of text by itself at the top of a page. An **orphan** is a single line by itself at the bottom of a page. You can prohibit such single lines or specify how many lines of a paragraph must appear on any page.

If your program uses a widow/orphan protection command, it will move any single line of text that occurs at the bottom of a page to the top of the next page. When a single line occurs at the top of a page, WordPerfect moves a line from the previous page to join that line.

Using a Hard Page Break

126

A **hard page break** is not readjusted as you insert or delete text on the page. It stays with the text where you entered it. A hard page break might be used to end a title page because you would probably always want that page to end at the same spot.

A hard page break gives you control over the page endings, but you give up automatic adjustment. You can still insert or delete text on the page, but the hard page break does not move. When you type a report that flows continuously from page to page, soft page breaks are best. If you type five separate letters in a document, each to a different person, hard page breaks keep each individual's letter on its own page.

TUTORIAL

In this tutorial, you append one document to another to create a document that is longer than one page. You see the soft page break and insert/delete text to reposition it. You use the Block/Protect and Widow/Orphan Protection commands to adjust page endings. You also insert and delete a hard page break.

Beginning with this topic, you are no longer reminded to change the directory and insert your document disk.

1 Create a long document. Retrieve EXER11A from your disk.

Select	"Edit," "Block"	Displays "Block on."
Press	PAGE DOWN	Blocks page.
Select	"Edit," "Append," "To File"	Displays "Append to."

You can execute the Block/Append command from the keyboard with the Control-F4 key.

Type	exer13a	Enters filename.

This is the file to which the block is appended.

Press	↵ ENTER	Appends blocked text.
Select	"File," "Exit," "No," "No"	Clears screen.
Select	"File," "Retrieve"	Displays Retrieve prompt.
Type	exer13a	Enters filename.
Press	↵ ENTER	Retrieves EXER13A.
Select	"Layout," "Line," "Margins"	Moves cursor to left margin field.

Change the left and right margins to 1.5 inches and return to the document. You can execute the Left/Right Margin command from the keyboard with the Shift-F8 key.

Select	"Font," "Base Font"	Displays fonts list.

Use a font similar to 10-pitch Courier if your list does not include Courier. You can execute the Font command from the keyboard with the Control-F8 key.

Select	"Courier 10 cpi"	Changes font.
Select	"Search," "Replace"	Displays "w/Confirm?"
Select	"No"	Displays "-> Srch:".
Press	CTRL-F8	Enters search string.

You must use the keyboard command to enter the initial code in a search string.

Select	"Size"	Displays Size menu.

Select the font size that you use for titles.

Select	"Ext Large" or "Vry Large"	Displays search string.
Press	F2	Displays "Replace with?"
Press	F2	Replaces font codes.

Font size codes are replaced with nothing; they are deleted. This helps your document match the instructions.

Press	HOME twice, ↑	Moves cursor to page 1.
Select	"Search," "Forward"	Displays "-> Srch:".

Use Search to position the cursor to a specific location, at "Altonia" with a question mark.

Type	Altonia?	Enters search string.
Press	F2	Moves cursor to end of first document.
Press	↵ ENTER twice	Inserts blank lines.

Use a triple space or two blank lines between the documents. You need three [HRt] codes between the documents as shown in Figure 15.1. Reveal codes to check, then remove the Codes screen.

Figure 15.1
Insert Hard Returns to Separate Documents

```
     easy accessibility and reduced chance of injury.

     Breakaway rearview mirror.  The mirror is designed to
     break away from the windshield if hit with moderate
     force.

For more information call 1-800-900-1111 or visit your nearest
dealer.  Isn't it time you traded up to Altonia?


                  WAYS TO REDUCE STRESS
A:\EXER13A                                   Doc 1 Pg 1 Ln 4.83" Pos 1"
For more information call 1[-]800[-]900[-]1111 or visit your nearest[SRt]
dealer.  Isn't it time you traded up to Altonia?[HRt]
[HRt]
[HRt]
[Center]WAYS TO REDUCE STRESS[HRt]
[HRt]
[Tab Set:Rel: -1",-0.5",+0.5",+1"]As a student, an employee, and a family member
, you are subject[SRt]
to many stressful situations.  Learn to take things in stride by[SRt]
observing a few simple principles.[HRt]

Press Reveal Codes to restore screen
```

hard returns inserted

TIP A soft page code is inserted when a space or a soft return [SRt] ends the page. A [HRt-SPg] code is inserted when a hard return ends the page. If a hard return is the first code after a soft page break, the [HRt] is converted to a dormant hard return [Dorm HRt] so that it does not print a blank line at the beginning of the page.

2 Work with soft page breaks.

Press	HOME three times, ↑	Moves cursor to top of document.
Press	CTRL-HOME, ↓	Moves cursor to bottom of page 1.
Press	↓	Moves cursor to top of page 2.

A soft page break is a single dashed line and [SPg] in the Codes screen. ◀

Press	F11	Displays Codes screen.

Look for an [SPg] or [HRt-SPg] code at the end of page 1.

Press	F11	Removes Codes screen.

Watch the screen to determine how many times to press the Up Arrow to position the cursor at item 3 at the left margin.

Press	↑	Moves cursor to Pos 1.5" with item 3.
Select	"Edit," "Block"	Displays "Block on."
Press	↵ ENTER, ↓	Blocks item 3 and blank line.

Press	DELETE	Displays "Delete block?"
Select	"Yes"	Deletes block.

The text previously on page 2 is now on page 1.

Select	"Edit," "Undelete," "Restore"	Restores paragraph and page break.

Watch the screen to determine how many times to press the Up Arrow to position the cursor at item 3 at the left margin.

Press	↑	Moves cursor to Pos 1.5".
Press	↵ ENTER	Inserts [HRt] code.

It is easier to add a new paragraph if you first insert a blank line.

Press	↑	Moves cursor to blank line.
Press	TAB	Indents paragraph.
Type	3.	Enters number and period.
Select	"Layout," "Align," "Indent -> <-"	Indents paragraph from both margins.

Type the following paragraph.

```
3. Manage your time in accordance with your
   goals. You'll be able to accomplish more
   with less effort.
```

Press	↵ ENTER	Ends paragraph.

The page break is adjusted as you type. The original paragraph 3 is split between pages. Watch the screen to determine how many times to press the Down and Right Arrows to position the cursor to change the original number 3 to 4.

Press	↓, →	Moves cursor to 3.

Change the number to 4 so that the paragraph is properly numbered.

3 **Use Block Protect.** EXER13A is still on the screen. Watch the screen to determine how many times to press the Left Arrow to move the cursor to Pos 1.5" with item 4.

Press	←	Moves cursor to Pos 1.5".
Select	"Edit," "Block"	Displays "Block on."

> **TIP** Use Block Protect for lines that must always stay together. You can insert or delete text within the block. This is especially important with tables and charts.

> **TIP** WordPerfect has a Conditional End of Page command which keeps a specified number of lines together. Count the lines, including blank lines. Then select "Layout," "Other," and "Conditional End of Page," and type the number of lines to be kept together.

Press	↵ ENTER	Blocks item 4.
Select	"Edit," "Protect Block"	Inserts new soft page break.

The page break is inserted before the block to keep the lines together. ◀

Press	F11	Displays Codes screen.

Look for the [Block Pro:On] and [Block Pro:Off] codes.

Press	F11	Removes Codes screen.

You can execute the Block/Protect command from the keyboard with the Shift-F8 key after the Block command is started. ◀

4 Use Widow/Orphan Protection. EXER13A is still on the screen. Position the cursor after the period at the end of item 3.

Press	SPACEBAR twice	Inserts two spaces.

Type the following paragraph. The page break will appear as you type.

```
At the end of each day, you will be able to relax if you do
not have so many things left unattended. A soothing, calm
feeling of peace will pervade.
```

The last line of the paragraph should be the first line of page 2, an orphan line. If your screen does not appear like this, your font is different and causes the break to appear in another location. Insert a word or two to force the creation of an orphan line. If you still cannot create an orphan line, your default may have been changed to use Widow/Orphan Protection all the time.

Figure 15.2
Orphan Line and Page Break

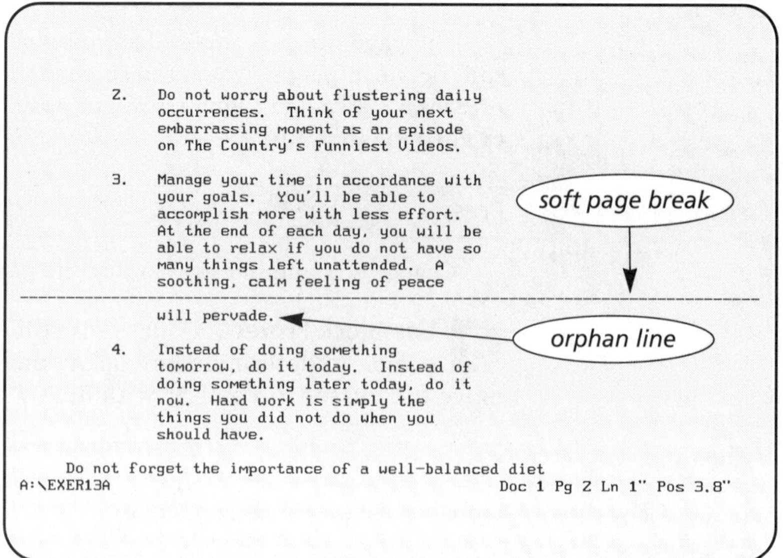

Press	HOME twice, ↑	Moves cursor to beginning of document.
Select	"Layout," "Line"	Displays Line Format.
Select	"Widow/Orphan Protection"	Moves cursor to option.
Select	"Yes"	Returns cursor to Selection line.
Press	F7	Returns to document.
Press	F11	Displays [W/O On] code.

If your default is "Yes" for Widow/Orphan Protection, you will not see a [W/O On] code even if you selected "Yes."

Press	F11	Removes Codes screen.
Press	PAGE DOWN	Moves cursor to top of page 2.

WordPerfect positions the soft page break so that there are no orphan lines. You can execute the Widow/Orphan Protection command from the keyboard with the Shift-F8 key.

5 **Use a hard page break.** The cursor is at the top of page 2 in EXER13A.

Select	"Search," "Backward"	Displays "<- Srch:".
Press	↵ ENTER three times	Enters search string.
Press	F2	Moves cursor.

> **TIP** If you add or delete text from a page with a hard page break, check the page break to determine if it is still in a desirable location. A hard page break is not adjusted automatically.

The three hard returns are between the two documents.

Press	CTRL-↵ ENTER	Inserts hard page break.

A hard page break is a double dashed line and [HPg] in the Codes screen. ◀

Press	F11	Displays [HPg] code.
Press	F11	Removes Codes screen.
Press	←BACKSPACE	Deletes hard page break.
Select	"File," "Exit," "No," "No"	Clears screen.

PROCEDURE SUMMARY

USING SOFT PAGE BREAKS

Set the desired top and side margins.	
Type the document.	(your input)

KEEPING LINES TOGETHER ON A PAGE

Block the text to be kept together.	
Activate the menu bar.	ALT - =
Select "Edit."	E
Select "Protect Block."	T

USING WIDOW/ORPHAN PROTECTION

Position the cursor where Widow/Orphan Protection should start.	
Activate the menu bar.	ALT - =
Select "Layout."	L
Select "Line."	L
Select "Widow/Orphan Protection."	W or 9
Select "Yes."	Y
Return to the document.	F7

USING A HARD PAGE BREAK

To insert a hard page break:

Position the cursor where the new page is to begin.	
Insert the hard page break.	CTRL - ↵ENTER

To delete a hard page break:

Position the cursor below the double dashed line.	
Delete the hard page break.	←BACKSPACE

EXERCISES

15A **Complete the following tasks:**

1. Type the following document. Turn on Widow/Orphan Protection at the top of the page.

GLOBAL HOTEL
VANCOUVER, BRITISH COLUMBIA

Subject Property

The subject property consists of a deluxe 50-story hotel located on the Avenue Sterling in Vancouver. This building contains 450 guest rooms, conference facilities, 7 restaurants, and extensive banquet rooms.

The hotel opened in 1989 and is managed by Mitok Corporation.

Location

Global Hotel is situated on the Avenue Sterling across from Park Place and the Tokyo Hotel in the modern city of Vancouver in the Province of British Columbia, Canada.

The population of the Vancouver metropolitan area has grown steadily during the 1980s. It is estimated that over 1.5 million people now live within 75 square miles of the city. Vancouver itself has a population of about 550,000 with an effective buying power in excess of $45,000 per household.

As a tourist destination, Vancouver receives most of its visitors during the summer months. It is estimated that 350,000 tourists visited the city during the summer of 1990. Vancouver enjoys a fair amount of visitors during the winter months also because of the nearby ski resorts.

Vancouver is served by several major expressways linking it with Seattle and the eastern part of Canada. New and improved highways continue to be constructed as the city grows.

Structure

The architectural design is contemporary and emphasizes the exterior facade of marble and glass. The unique design of reinforced concrete incorporates alternating concrete walls as firewalls throughout the hotel.

There are four subground floors and 50 stories above ground. The rectangular shape includes a sloping wall on the west side from the fifth to the tenth floors.

All construction conforms to Vancouver city building specifications.

2. Center each title line and use a very large font size. End the font size after the second title line. Double space after the titles.
3. Change to double spacing before the first side heading. Use Bold, Italic, or Underline for the side headings. A soft page break will be inserted when you reach the bottom margin, near Ln 10".
4. Use Spell.
5. Save your document as EXER15A. Print using Full Document to print both pages.

15B Complete the following tasks:

1. Retrieve EXER15A.
2. Insert the following paragraph so that it appears after the paragraph that begins "Global Hotel is situated . . ."

```
     Vancouver is located in the southwestern section of the
Province with a well-developed commercial and recreational
harbor on the Pacific Ocean.
```

3. Press HOME three times and then press UP to position the cursor at the top of page 1. Make sure the cursor is on the first code.
4. Insert a hard page break as the first code. An empty page 1 is created.
5. Position the cursor on page 1. Give the Center Page (top to bottom) command.
6. Start the very large font size. Center and type the following lines.

NEW HOTEL PROPERTIES
FISCAL YEAR
PREPARED BY
YOUR NAME

7. End the font size.
8. Resave the document as EXER15A. Print using Full Document.

Using Page Numbers

CONCEPTS Printed page numbers are important in any long document so that you can refer to various parts of the work. With a Page Numbering command, you select what kind of numbers you want, where numbers print on the page, and what number should start the numbering.

Starting Page Numbers 133

Page numbers do not print on the page unless you give the command. You normally give the Page Numbering command on the page where the first page number should print. If the first few pages of a document are the title and table of contents pages, you may not want to start printed numbering until page 3.

In WordPerfect, you can select from Arabic or upper- or lowercase Roman numerals. Page numbers are not visible in the regular screen; you need to use the View mode.

Changing the Page Number 

Pages are numbered consecutively, beginning with the number you specify or the default. If you are working on an article that will be page 12 in a book, start the numbering with 12 instead of 1. This allows you to keep sections of a long document in separate files but number them as a whole.

The default number is the actual page number in the document. If it is page 4 in your document, the printed number will be 4. If the title page is page 1 in a document, page 2 is the first page of text to be numbered.

Choosing a Page Number Position 

Page numbers can be positioned at the top or bottom margins, at the left or right edges, or in the center. It is customary to place page numbers for even and odd pages as mirrors of each other. For example, right-hand page numbers print at the right margin, and left-hand page numbers print at the left margin.

The printed position is based on the paper size and the margins. You may need to experiment to see where your software places the page number. If your top margin is 1 inch, the page number may print at the margin. Some software may print the number above the top margin, about 0.5 inch from the top. There may also be default blank space above or below the page number to separate it from the text.

Stopping the Page Numbers

134

Page numbers continue until the end of the document or until you stop them. If you have a landscape page in the middle of your work, you do not want the page number to print on that page. It would not match the other pages because the print is across the wide side of the paper.

Your software may allow you to stop the page numbers for a single page and have them restarted on the next page. You may also be able to stop page numbering from any page forward.

TUTORIAL

In this tutorial, you number the pages of a document. You choose the page number position, change the page number, and suppress the number.

1 Start page numbers.

Retrieve EXER15A from your disk.

Press	PAGE DOWN	Moves cursor to top of page 2.
Select	"Layout," "Page"	Displays Page Format menu.
Select	"Page Numbering"	Displays Page Numbering menu.

There are now no page numbers.

Select	"Page Number Position"	Displays numbering options.

There are nine selections available from the Page Number Position menu as shown in Figure 16.1.

Figure 16.1
Page Number Position Menu

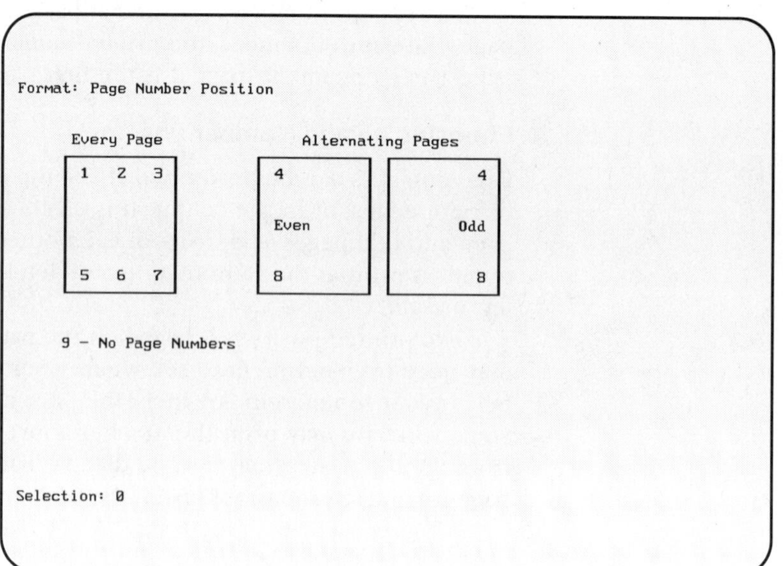

Select	7	Chooses number position.

This prints numbers at the bottom right corner of every page.

Press	F7	Returns to document.

You can execute the Page Numbering command from the keyboard with the Shift-F8 key.

Press	F11	Displays [Pg Numbering: Bottom Right] code.
Press	F11	Removes Codes screen.
Select	"File," "Print," "View Document"	Displays View screen.

The page number is visible in the View screen. If need be, press 3 for Full Page view.

Press	PAGE DOWN	Displays next page.
Press	PAGE UP twice	Displays title page.

The title page does not have a printed page number.

Press	PAGE DOWN	Displays next page.

The first page of text is numbered as page 2.

Press	SPACEBAR	Displays Print menu.
Select	"Full Document"	Prints document.

Page numbers print at the bottom margin with one blank line before the number.

Select	"File," "Save"	Displays current filename.
Press	↵ ENTER	Displays Replace prompt.
Select	"Yes"	Resaves EXER15A.

2 Change the page number position and the page number.

EXER15A should be on the screen.

Press	F11	Displays Codes screen.

Watch the screen and position the cursor on the [Pg Numbering: Bottom Right] code.

Press	DELETE	Deletes page numbering.
Select	"Layout," "Page," "Page Numbering"	Displays Page Numbering menu.

There are no page numbers now. You must select a page number position for a page number to print.

Select	"Page Number Position"	Displays numbering options.

Choose any option that will print numbers on "Every Page."

Select	(your input)	Displays Page Numbering menu.
Select	"New Page Number"	Moves cursor to field.
Type	1	Changes starting number.
Press	↵ ENTER	Moves cursor to Selection line.
Press	F7	Returns to document.

Look for the [Pg Numbering: Position] and [Pg Num:1] codes. When you use a New Page Number, the status line shows that new number.

Press	F11	Removes Codes screen.
Select	"File," "Print," "View Document"	Displays page 1.

The first page of text is now numbered 1.

Press	PAGE DOWN	Displays second text page.
Press	PAGE UP twice	Displays unnumbered title page.
Press	SPACEBAR twice	Returns to document.
Select	"File," "Save"	Displays current filename.
Press	↵ ENTER	Displays Replace prompt.
Select	"Yes"	Resaves EXER15A.

3 **Suppress the page number.** EXER15A should be on the screen.

Press	F11	Displays Codes screen.

Watch the screen and position the cursor on the [Pg Numbering] code.

Select	"Layout," "Page"	Displays Page Format menu.

Select	"Suppress (this page only)"	Displays Suppress menu.
Select	"Suppress Page Numbering," "Yes"	Returns cursor to Selection line.
Press	F7	Returns to document.

Look for the [Suppress:PgNum] code. You can execute the Suppress command from the keyboard with the Shift-F8 key.

> **TIP** The Suppress command affects the current page. To stop the page numbers from printing from the current page forward, select No Page Numbering from the Page Number options.

Press	F11	Removes Codes screen.
Select	"File," "Print," "View Document"	Displays first page.

The page number is suppressed on the first page of text. ◀

Press	PAGE DOWN	Displays next page.

Page numbering resumes on the next page.

Press	SPACEBAR	Displays Print menu.
Select	"Full Document"	Prints document.
Select	"File," "Exit," "Yes"	Displays Save prompt.
Press	↵ ENTER	Displays Replace prompt.
Select	"Yes," "No"	Resaves EXER15A and clears screen.

PROCEDURE SUMMARY

STARTING PAGE NUMBERS

Position the cursor at the top of the page where numbers should start.	
Activate the menu bar.	ALT - =
Select "Layout."	L
Select "Page."	P
Select "Page Numbering."	N
Select "Page Number Position."	P
Choose a location.	(your input)
Return to the document.	F7

CHANGING THE PAGE NUMBER

Position the cursor at the top of the page where numbers should start or be changed.	
Activate the menu bar.	ALT-=
Select "Layout."	L
Select "Page."	P
Select "Page Numbering."	N
Select "New Page Number."	N
Type a new number.	(your input)
Accept number.	↵ ENTER
Return to the document.	F7

CHOOSING A PAGE NUMBER POSITION

Position the cursor at the top of the page where numbers should start or be changed.	
Delete any existing [Pg Numbering] code.	DELETE
Activate the menu bar.	ALT-=
Select "Layout."	L
Select "Page."	P
Select "Page Numbering."	N
Select "Page Number Position."	P
Choose a location.	(your input)
Return to the document.	F7

STOPPING THE PAGE NUMBERS

Position the cursor on the page where numbers should be stopped.	
Activate the menu bar.	ALT-=
Select "Layout."	L
Select "Page."	P
Select "Suppress."	U
Choose the page numbering option.	P or 4
Select "Yes."	Y
Return to the document.	F7

EXERCISES

16A **Complete the following tasks:**

1. Type the following document. Turn on Widow/Orphan Protection at the top of the page.

DIS, DAT, AND DOS
by
Bink Burke

```
   It happened quite suddenly, a computer was given to me. My
children presented it Christmas Eve. It looked so harmless, you
just would not believe!
   You must go to school and study DOS, said my son, and then
you will be smarter than anyone. How exciting I said with joy.
This is such fun, like a new toy.
   There is A: and B: and really hard C. There is format and
copy and xcopy, too. Just delete everything if you don't know
what to do.
   There's a path that goes nowhere without a colon; put it in
AUTOEXEC.BAT so it won't get stolen. There is one dot and two
dots and back and forth slashes. There is even a tree with a
root and branches!
   Then came commands that were external and more that were
internal. Why there is even a board known as maternal. But the
command that I most often see is ABORT, RETRY, OR WE WILL FAIL
THEE!
   There are batch files and botched files and hidden files,
too. I can't look for them now, I have too much to do.
   Just make a directory with a bit of MD; you can change it
later when you type CD. There is PROMPT with $ signs that don't
stand for money. Now don't you think that's a little bit funny?
   Is it morning or night? I have been here so long, but my work
is finished to my great delight. I wish all my classmates could
see me now. They would all clap as I take a bow.
   But they have all gone home, and there is no one about. Hope
I can get the printer to spit my work out. Online, then Offline,
then tap and hold. Must get this right so teacher won't scold.

   Patiently I wait for my paper to appear, but not a sound from
the printer do I hear. Back to the computer to give a command. I
want my printout, I demand! But the message I read makes me want
to punch. "You forgot FEED and MENU, I've gone out to lunch."
```

2. Start page numbering to number every page in the upper right corner.
3. Center the title lines and use a large font size. End the font size after the third title line. Press ENTER twice.

4. Change to double spacing after the title lines. A soft page break will be inserted when you reach the bottom margin, near Ln 10".
5. Use Spell. View your work.
6. Save your document as EXER16A. Print the Full Document.

16B Complete the following tasks:

1. Retrieve EXER16A.
2. Delete the [Pg Numbering] code.
3. Change the page number of page 1 to page 10 and use page numbers that print at the bottom center of every page.
4. View your work and print the full document.
5. Do not resave your document.

Using Headers and Footers

CONCEPTS Headers and footers are used to display information like company names, a date, or maybe a chapter title. A header is text that appears at the top of every page of a long document. A footer is text that appears at the bottom of every page. These items are repeated throughout the document, but you type them only once as the header or footer.

Creating a Header or Footer

142

A Header or Footer command is placed on the page where it should start. If the header includes your company name, you may want it to start on page 2 if the first page is printed on company letterhead.

You can position header or footer text at the left margin, in the center, or at the right. Many software programs allow you to indicate whether headers or footers should be on every page, on just the odd pages, or on just the even pages. A header for an even-numbered page might be different from the header for the odd-numbered page. You might use left alignment for the even pages but right alignment for the odd pages.

Like page numbers, headers and footers are usually not visible in the regular screen; you need to use View mode to see them. Headers and footers may be positioned at the top and bottom margins with a predetermined amount of space before or after each. In WordPerfect 5.1, headers and footers are part of the text and they print above or below the margins.

Pagination in WordPerfect takes headers and footers into account. When you add a header or a footer to a page, fewer lines of the actual document fit on the page. If a word processing program does not recognize the space required for the header/footer, you need to make sure there are not too many lines per page.

Many software packages allow you to use a header or a footer to number the pages, too. When you do so, you can include additional text so that the header or footer appears like this: "DIS, DAT, and DOS - Page 1." 

> **TIP** If you use a header or a footer to number the pages, do not use a separate Page Numbering command. For a header/footer to include page numbering, type ^B (CTRL-B) at the point where a page number should print.

Editing a Header or Footer

142

In WordPerfect, the header/footer screen is a special editing window where you type what you want as the header/footer. You can add styles such as underline, bold, or italic. In some word processors, the header or footer may be limited to a certain number of lines. Many packages, however, allow you to make the header or footer as long as you like.

You can usually insert, delete, move, copy, and replace in a header/footer. If you use the Spell checking ability of your software, you need to determine whether or not it checks the spelling of the header/footer in addition to the main document; WordPerfect does.

Suppressing a Header or Footer

143

Headers and footers start on the page where they are created. They continue until the end of the document or until you stop them. For the same reasons that you might want to suppress page numbers, you might want to discontinue a header/footer. A title page, a table of contents, and an appendix might not need the same header/footer as the rest of the document.

Your software may allow you to stop the header/footer for a single page and have it be restarted on the next page. You may also be able to discontinue or delete the header/footer for the rest of the document.

TUTORIAL

In this tutorial, you add a footer to a document. You delete the footer and add a header. Then you suppress the header for the first page.

1 **Create a footer.** Retrieve EXER16A from your disk. A header or footer must be inserted before any text. Otherwise, it takes effect on the next page.

Select	"Layout," "Page"	Displays Page Format menu.
Select	"Footers"	Displays Footer menu.

You can have two footers in a document.

Select	"Footer A"	Displays Footer A menu.

Footers can appear on different pages, be discontinued, or be edited.

Select	"Every Page"	Displays editing window.
Select	"Layout," "Align," "Flush Right"	Moves cursor to right margin.
Type	DIS, DAT, and DOS	Enters footer text.
Press	F7	Removes editing window.

The Page Format menu shows that Footer A will appear on every page.

Press	F7	Returns to document.
Press	F11	Displays [Footer A] code.

> **TIP** A footer/header code displays the first 100 characters of the text in the footer/header. When there are more than 100 characters in the footer/header, you will see "..." at the end of the code.

You can execute the Footer command from the keyboard with the Shift-F8 key. ◀

Press	F11	Removes Codes screen.
Select	"File," "Print," "View Document"	Displays View screen.

The footer appears on the first page at the bottom margin.

Press	PAGE DOWN	Displays next page.
Press	SPACEBAR	Displays Print menu.
Select	"Full Document"	Prints document.
Select	"File," "Save"	Displays Save prompt.
Press	END	Moves cursor to end of filename.
Press	←BACKSPACE twice	Deletes 6A.
Type	7a	Changes filename.
Press	↵ENTER	Saves EXER17A.

2 **Delete a footer and add a header.** EXER17A should be on the screen.

Press	PAGE UP	Moves cursor to top of page 1.
Press	F11	Displays Codes screen.

Watch the screen and position the cursor on the [Footer A] code.

Press	DELETE	Deletes footer.
Select	"Layout," "Page," "Headers"	Displays Header menu.
Select	"Header A"	Displays Header A menu.
Select	"Every Page"	Displays header editing window.

The editing window appears with the codes revealed because the codes are revealed in the document.

Type	EXER17A	Enters header at left margin.
Press	F7	Removes header window.

The Page Format menu shows that Header A will appear on every page.

Press	F7	Returns to document.

Press	F11	Removes Codes screen.
Select	"File," "Print," "View Document"	Displays View screen.

The header and page numbering appear on the first page at the top margin.

Press	PAGE DOWN	Displays next page.
Press	SPACEBAR	Displays Print menu.
Select	"Full Document"	Prints document.
Select	"File," "Save"	Displays current filename.
Press	↵ ENTER	Displays Replace prompt.
Select	"Yes"	Resaves EXER17A.

You can execute the Header command from the keyboard with the Shift-F8 key.

3 **Suppress the header.** EXER17A should be on the screen.

Press	PAGE UP	Moves cursor to top of page 1.
Press	F11	Displays Codes screen.

Watch the screen and position the cursor on the [Header A] code.

Select	"Layout," "Page," "Suppress"	Displays Suppress menu.

You can suppress several combinations of page numbers and headers/footers as shown in Figure 17.1.

Select	"Suppress Header A," "Yes"	Changes option.
Press	F7	Returns to document.

A [Suppress:HA] code has been inserted.

Press	F11	Removes Codes screen.
Select	"File," "Print," "View Document"	Displays View screen.

Only page numbering appears on page 1. The header is suppressed on page 1.

Press	PAGE DOWN	Displays next page.

The header and the page numbering appear on page 2. ◀

TIP When you suppress a header or a footer, it is stopped for the current page but resumes on the next page. You can stop a header or footer for the rest of a document by selecting "Discontinue" at the Header/Footer menu.

Figure 17.1
Suppress Menu

```
Format: Suppress (this page only)

     1 - Suppress All Page Numbering, Headers and Footers

     2 - Suppress Headers and Footers

     3 - Print Page Number at Bottom Center   No

     4 - Suppress Page Numbering              No

     5 - Suppress Header A                    No

     6 - Suppress Header B                    No

     7 - Suppress Footer A                    No

     8 - Suppress Footer B                    No



Selection: 0
```

Press	SPACEBAR twice	Returns to document.
Select	"File," "Save"	Displays filename.
Press	↵ ENTER	Displays Replace prompt.
Select	"Yes"	Resaves EXER17A.

You can execute the Suppress command from the keyboard with the Shift-F8 key.

4 **Edit a header.** EXER17A should be on the screen.

Press	PAGE UP	Moves cursor to top of page 1.
Select	"Layout," "Page," "Headers"	Displays Header menu.
Select	"Header A"	Displays Header A menu.
Select	"Edit"	Displays header editing window.
Press	CTRL-END	Deletes line.
Select	"Font," "Appearance"	Displays Appearance menu.

You can use font sizes or appearances in a header or a footer. Use italic or shadow print.

Select	(your input)	Inserts codes.
Type	DIS, DAT, and DOS	Enters header text.
Press	→	Ends font appearance.

Press	F7 twice	Returns to document.
Select	"File," "Print," "View Document"	Displays View screen.

The [Suppress:HA] code is on page 1. The header and the page numbering appear on page 2.

Press	PAGE DOWN	Displays next page.
Press	SPACEBAR	Displays Print menu.
Select	"Full Document"	Prints document.
Select	"File," "Exit," "Yes"	Displays Save prompt.
Press	↵ ENTER	Displays Replace prompt.
Select	"Yes," "No"	Resaves EXER17A and clears screen.

PROCEDURE SUMMARY

CREATING A HEADER OR FOOTER

Position the cursor at the top of the page where the header or footer should start.	
Activate the menu bar.	ALT - =
Select "Layout."	L
Select "Page."	P
Select "Headers" or "Footers."	H or F
Create the first header or footer.	A or 1
Select the frequency for the header or footer.	P or O or V
Type the text for the header or footer.	(your input)
Exit the editing window.	F7

EDITING A HEADER OR FOOTER

Activate the menu bar.	ALT - =
Select "Layout."	L
Select "Page."	P

Select "Headers" or "Footers."	H or F
Select the first or second header or footer.	A or B
Select "Edit."	E
Change the text.	(your input)
Exit the editing window.	F7

SUPPRESSING A HEADER OR FOOTER

Position the cursor at the top of the page where the header or footer should stop.	
Activate the menu bar.	ALT-=
Select "Layout."	L
Select "Page."	P
Select "Suppress."	U
Select the option to be suppressed.	(your input)

EXERCISES

17A **Complete the following tasks:**

1. Retrieve EXER17A.
2. Delete the [Suppress:HA] code, the [Header A] code, and the [Pg Numbering] code.
3. Make sure the cursor is on the first character or code in the document.
4. Create a new Footer A to appear on every page.
5. Select "Layout," "Align," and "Flush Right" to position the footer text.
6. Hold down Control and type B. "^B" will appear on the screen.
7. Exit the footer window and view the document.
8. Print the full document.
9. Resave your work as EXER17A.

17B Complete the following tasks:

1. Retrieve EXER15A.
2. Delete all page numbering codes on page 2.
3. On page 1, create Header A to appear on every page.
4. Select "Layout," "Align," and "Center" to center the header text.
5. Type the word "Page." Press the SPACEBAR once.
6. Hold down Control and type B. "^B" will appear on the screen.
7. Exit the header window and view the document.
8. Suppress the header on page 1.
9. On page 2, change to a New Page Number 1.
10. Print the full document.
11. Resave your work as EXER15A.

Using Footnotes

CONCEPTS A footnote is used to list a source of information or to provide more detail about something in the text. In a technical report, you might include footnotes to explain where you found your research data. Word processing software places and numbers footnotes for you.

Creating a Footnote (150)

A footnote consists of a reference number within the text, usually superscripted, and the corresponding explanation, usually at the bottom of the same page. When you create a footnote, you mark the location in the text where the reference is made. Then you type the text for the footnote. In WordPerfect, footnotes are typed in an editing window similar to what you use for a header or a footer. You can create a footnote as the document is typed or after you have finished.

When you create a footnote, the software assigns the next number and places the footnote at the bottom margin. Footnotes are numbered consecutively beginning with number 1, but you may be able to change the starting number. The text on each page is reduced to fit the margins as you add footnotes, so you need not worry about leaving enough space for the footnotes. WordPerfect inserts a horizontal divider rule followed by a blank line between the footnotes and the text. ◀

> **TIP** WordPerfect has footnotes and endnotes. Footnotes are placed at the bottom of the page; endnotes are gathered in one location, usually at the end of the document. A document can have both footnotes and endnotes.

Since numbering is automatic, you can add or delete footnotes whenever necessary. If you move text that contains a footnote reference, it is moved with the text and renumbered according to its new position.

Like headers and footers, footnotes may not be visible on the regular screen; you need to use the View mode. Various default options, which you may wish to change, will likely affect the appearance of footnotes. These options include the position of the number, what type of number is used, and the length of the horizontal rule.

Editing a Footnote (151)

Like headers and footers, footnotes can be edited as needed. You can insert, delete, move, and copy footnote text. You can also use styles such as bold or italic. Footnotes can be as long as necessary, but the text on the page is reduced accordingly. In WordPerfect, Spell checks footnote spelling, too.

Deleting a Footnote (151)

If you delete the fifth footnote in a document that has ten footnotes, the remaining footnotes are automatically renumbered. Both the reference number in the text and the number with the footnote are updated.

You can also insert a footnote with automatic renumbering. You just need to position the cursor at the reference point and create the new footnote.

TIP If you copy text with a footnote, a duplicate of the footnote is created with the next number. Make sure this is what you intend to do.

Moving a Footnote

(151)

You can move either a footnote reference or the block of text that contains it. To move a footnote reference, move only the reference code. You might do this if you decided that the reference was more important in a different location. If moved or copied paragraphs contain footnotes, the footnotes are also moved/copied. The numbers are updated, and the pages are adjusted to make room for the footnote text. ◀

TUTORIAL

In this tutorial, you add footnotes to a document. You edit a footnote, delete a footnote, and move a footnote.

1 Create a footnote. Retrieve EXER16A from your disk.

Select	"Search," "Forward"	Displays "-> Srch:".
Type	me	Enters search string.
Press	F2	Moves cursor to "me."
Select	"Layout," "Footnote"	Displays Footnote menu.
Select	"Create"	Displays editing window.

The footnote editing window displays the first number as shown in Figure 18.1. Type the following sentence.

```
Bink Burke is a student at Palos Valley College and a
resident of Evergreen Park, Illinois.
```

Figure 18.1

Footnote Window with First Footnote Text

```
    1Bink Burke is a student at Palos Valley College and a
resident of Evergreen Park, Illinois.

Footnote: Press Exit when done              Doc 1 Pg 1 Ln 1.67" Pos 4.7"
```

Press	F7	Returns to document.

The footnote number appears in the text. Printed footnote numbers are superscripted in the text and the footnote.

Select	"File," "Print," "View Document"	Displays footnote at bottom margin.

Use a Full Page view to see the footnotes. You can execute the Footnote command from the keyboard with the Control-F7 key.

Press	SPACEBAR twice	Returns to document.
Press	F11	Displays Codes screen.

Look for the [Footnote] code. The beginning portion of the footnote is displayed in the code.

Press	F11	Removes Codes screen.
Select	"Search," "Forward"	Displays "-> Srch:".
Type	dos	Enters search string.

Type lowercase letters to search for all occurrences of the word "DOS."

Press	F2	Moves cursor to "DOS."
Select	"Layout," "Footnote," "Create"	Displays window with next number.

Type the following sentence.

```
DOS is an acronym for Disk Operating System.
```

Press	F7	Returns to document.
Select	"File," "Print," "View Document"	Displays both footnotes at bottom margin.
Press	SPACEBAR	Returns to document.
Select	"File," "Save"	Displays filename.
Press	END	Moves cursor to end of filename.
Press	←BACKSPACE twice	Deletes 6A.
Type	8a	Changes filename.
Press	↵ENTER	Saves EXER18A.

2 **Edit a footnote.** EXER18A should be on the screen.

Select	"Layout," "Footnote," "Edit"	Displays "Footnote number?"

The prompt shows the next available number. You can edit any footnote by typing its number.

Type	1	Enters footnote number.
Press	↵ ENTER	Displays first footnote window.
Press	CTRL-→	Moves cursor to "C" in "College."
Type	Community	Inserts "Community."
Press	SPACEBAR	Inserts space.
Press	F7	Returns to document.
Select	"File," "Print," "View Document"	Displays revised footnote.◀
Press	SPACEBAR twice	Returns to document.
Select	"File," "Save"	Displays filename.
Press	↵ ENTER	Displays Replace prompt.
Select	"Yes"	Resaves EXER18A.

TIP Change the size of the view if you want to see something more closely. Then use HOME/UP or HOME/DOWN to position the view to display the top or bottom of the page.

3 **Delete and insert a footnote.** EXER18A should be on the screen.

Select	"Search," "Forward"	Displays "-> Srch:".

You can search for the next footnote code. You must use keyboard commands to enter a search string.

Press	CTRL-F7	Displays footnote options.
Select	"Footnote"	Displays more options.
Select	"Note"	Enters [Footnote] as search string.
Press	F2	Moves cursor to next footnote.
Press	← BACKSPACE	Displays "Delete [Footnote:2]?"
Select	"Yes"	Deletes footnote.
Select	"File," "Print," "View Document"	Displays one footnote.
Press	SPACEBAR twice	Returns to document.
Select	"Edit," "Undelete," "Restore"	Restores footnote.
Select	"Search," "Backward"	Displays "<- Srch:".

Type	eve	Enters search string.
Press	F2	Moves cursor to "eve."
Select	"Search," "Backward"	Displays "<- Srch: eve".
Press	F2	Moves cursor to next occurrence.
Select	"Layout," "Footnote," "Create"	Displays window with appropriate number.

Type the following sentence: `Christmas Eve is December 24.`

Press	F7	Returns to document.

The new footnote number appears in the text. The screen is rewritten after the next command.

Select	"File," "Print," "View Document"	Displays three footnotes.
Press	SPACEBAR	Displays Print menu.
Select	"Full Document"	Prints document.
Select	"File," "Save"	Displays filename.
Press	↵ ENTER	Displays Replace prompt.
Select	"Yes"	Resaves EXER18A.

4 **Move a footnote.** EXER18A should be on the screen.

Select	"Search," "Forward"	Displays "<- Srch: eve".
Press	CTRL-F7	Displays footnote options.
Select	"Footnote"	Displays more options.
Select	"Note"	Enters [Footnote] as search string.
Press	F2	Moves cursor to comma after footnote.
Select	"Edit," "Block"	Displays "Block on."

TIP: If you do not have an enhanced keyboard, select "Edit, Move" to move the blocked text.

Block the footnote before giving the Move command. Position the cursor beneath the footnote number. ◀

Press	← twice	Blocks footnote number.
Press	CTRL-DELETE	Moves footnote to buffer memory.

Press	PAGE UP	Moves cursor to top to page.
Press	END	Moves cursor to end of title.
Press	↵ ENTER	Retrieves footnote.

The footnotes have been renumbered.

Select	"File," "Print," "View Document"	Displays three footnotes in new order.
Press	SPACEBAR twice	Returns to document.
Select	"Edit," "Block"	Displays "Block on."

Block the same footnote before giving the Move command. Position the cursor one position to the right of the footnote number.

Press	→	Blocks number.
Press	CTRL - DELETE	Moves footnote to buffer memory.
Select	"Search," "Forward"	Displays "-> Srch:".
Type	dos	Enters search string.
Press	F2	Moves cursor to "DOS."
Press	↵ ENTER	Retrieves footnote.
Press	DELETE	Deletes font size code.
Select	"File," "Print," "View Document"	Displays footnotes in new order.
Press	SPACEBAR twice	Returns to document.
Select	"File," "Save"	Displays filename.
Press	↵ ENTER	Displays Replace prompt.
Select	"Yes"	Resaves EXER18A.

PROCEDURE SUMMARY

CREATING A FOOTNOTE

Position the cursor at the location for the footnote reference.	
Activate the menu bar.	ALT - =
Select "Layout."	L

Select "Footnote."	F
Select "Create."	C
Type the footnote text.	(your input)
Exit the footnote window.	F7

EDITING A FOOTNOTE

Activate the menu bar.	ALT-=
Select "Layout."	L
Select "Footnote."	F
Select "Edit."	E
Type the number of the footnote to be edited.	(your input)
Accept the footnote number.	↵ ENTER
Edit the footnote.	(your input)
Exit the footnote window.	F7

DELETING A FOOTNOTE

To delete footnote when cursor is beneath the footnote reference number in the text:

Delete the footnote.	DELETE

To delete footnote when cursor is one position to the right of the footnote reference number:

Delete the footnote.	←BACKSPACE

MOVING A FOOTNOTE

Position the cursor beneath the footnote number in the text.	
Activate the menu bar.	ALT-=
Select "Edit."	E
Select "Block."	B
Block the footnote number.	(your input)
Start the Move command.	CTRL-DELETE
Position the cursor at the new location.	(your input)
Retrieve the footnote.	↵ ENTER

EXERCISES

18A Complete the following tasks:

1. Retrieve EXER13A.
2. Search for the word "bags."
3. Insert a footnote with the following text: "Air bags are manufactured to existing government safety standards."
4. Search for the word "controls."
5. Insert a footnote with the following text: "All controls are treated with special illumination properties."
6. View and print the document.
7. Resave your work as EXER13A.

18B Complete the following tasks:

1. Type the following document.

THE FACTS ABOUT CALCIUM

The importance of calcium in your diet is proven. It is essential to building and maintaining strong bones and teeth. Health authorities at the Global Academy of Sciences recommend that you get at least three calcium-rich servings a day for a total of 800 mg.[1]

Dairy products such as milk, yogurt, and cheese are good sources of calcium. Fortified orange juice and breakfast cereals include calcium as do dark, leafy vegetables. Since many people now try to reduce cholesterol and saturated fats in their diets, they have eliminated the traditional sources of calcium.

A new type of calcium included in many fortified fruit juices is known as ACB.[2] Independent studies have shown that ACB stops bone loss in elderly women and significantly strengthens bones in children.

[1]This study was published in the World Journal of Medicine.
[2]Absorbable Calcium Bicarbonate.

2. Center the title line and use a large font size. End the font size after the title line. Press ENTER twice.
3. Change to double spacing after the title line.
4. Insert the footnotes as you type the document.
5. Use Spell. View your work.
6. Save your document as EXER18B. Print a copy.

Preparing Form Letters

CONCEPTS

You have probably received many form letters or documents, such as letters from charitable organizations soliciting your help or from the school registration office reminding you to register for next semester. Form letters are timesavers because you only need to prepare one letter that can be personalized for as many people as necessary. Such letters are also helpful for responding to customers or clients who tend to ask the same questions or request the same information. You do not need to create a new letter for each person as long as one of your form letters fits their request.

Creating a Primary File

159

The process of preparing a form letter is often called "merge" because you combine two documents. A merge requires a primary document, which is the basic letter or memo that everyone receives. The primary file controls the merge and contains text and Merge commands (see Figure 19.1). The text in a primary file does not change from individual to individual.

Figure 19.1
Primary File to Be Created in Tasks

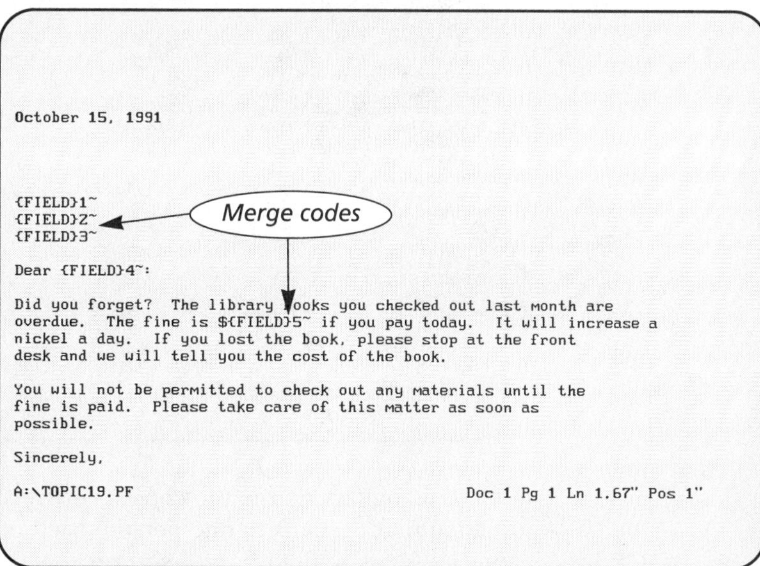

October 15, 1991

{FIELD}1~
{FIELD}2~
{FIELD}3~

Dear {FIELD}4~:

Did you forget? The library books you checked out last month are overdue. The fine is ${FIELD}5~ if you pay today. It will increase a nickel a day. If you lost the book, please stop at the front desk and we will tell you the cost of the book.

You will not be permitted to check out any materials until the fine is paid. Please take care of this matter as soon as possible.

Sincerely,

A:\TOPIC19.PF Doc 1 Pg 1 Ln 1.67" Pos 1"

TIP WordPerfect includes a merge programming language which allows you to carry out automatic routines within a merge. You can, for example, insert the current date and time with special Merge commands. You can create merge programs that test for certain conditions such as whether or not a customer owes money.

The primary file is typed and saved like any document. If you want all the letters to have 1.5-inch side margins, you place that code in the primary file. If there is a section with tabs, set the tabs in the letter and press Tab when necessary.

Merge commands must be placed carefully so that they do what you intend. The Merge commands identify "fields" or locations where text needs to be inserted. Merge commands extract information from a second file and insert it into the primary document to assemble a complete letter. If your Merge commands are wrong, you could end up with letters that say "Dear 123 Main Street." ◀

Merge commands in the letter may be numbered or named. You might number the name, address, and city as Fields "1," "2," and "3." Some word processors allow you to name the fields "Name," "Street Address," and "City." When you insert a Merge command in a sentence, space once before it and after it as if the text were there. If the inserted text would be followed by a hard return or a tab, type a tab or a hard return after the Merge command.

Creating a Secondary File 160

A secondary file includes the information necessary to complete a form letter. It can be a simple address list. It may be called a variable file because it contains text that varies from one letter to the next. The secondary file includes text and Merge commands (see Figure 19.2). As in the primary file, the placement of Merge commands is important.

Figure 19.2
Secondary File to Be Created in Tasks

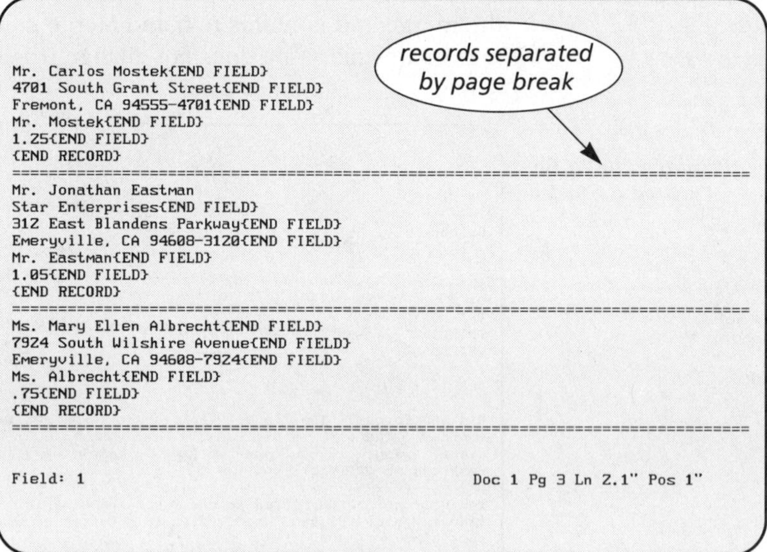

```
Mr. Carlos Mostek{END FIELD}
4701 South Grant Street{END FIELD}
Fremont, CA 94555-4701{END FIELD}
Mr. Mostek{END FIELD}
1.25{END FIELD}
{END RECORD}
================================================================================
Mr. Jonathan Eastman
Star Enterprises{END FIELD}
312 East Blandens Parkway{END FIELD}
Emeryville, CA 94608-3120{END FIELD}
Mr. Eastman{END FIELD}
1.05{END FIELD}
{END RECORD}
================================================================================
Ms. Mary Ellen Albrecht{END FIELD}
7924 South Wilshire Avenue{END FIELD}
Emeryville, CA 94608-7924{END FIELD}
Ms. Albrecht{END FIELD}
.75{END FIELD}
{END RECORD}
================================================================================

Field: 1                                        Doc 1 Pg 3 Ln 2.1" Pos 1"
```


A secondary merge file consists of "records." A record is all the information that pertains to one person. Each piece of information in the secondary file is a "field." Letters to prospective customers might have four fields: name, street address, city and state, and salutation. A bank sending a letter to overdrawn customers might use a secondary file with six fields: name, street address, city and state, salutation, account number, and amount of the overdraft.

> **TIP**
> WordPerfect's Merge commands can be used to create secondary files that are almost like database files. You can sort information in a secondary file as well as select certain records based on particular conditions.

Depending on your software, fields in the secondary file may be separated by a special command. Fields in a secondary file can be named or numbered, and they are usually entered in the order in which they are used in the letter.

Each record in a secondary document should have the same number of fields and the same type of information in that field. If the third field is the telephone number, each record should contain a telephone number at that point or be left blank. With most software, the information in a field is not limited to one line and can vary from one record to the next. Some persons might have a four-line address if their company name is included; others might have a three-line address. ◀

Printing Merge Letters

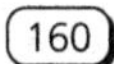

After the primary and secondary files are created and saved, they are merged into completed letters. If you have five records in the secondary file, five letters are created.

Some word processing packages merge directly to the printer. When you give the Merge command, the resulting document is printed immediately. If there are errors, you see them on the printed copies. Other packages merge the files on the screen, so you can correct errors before printing.

TUTORIAL

In this tutorial, you create primary and secondary files. Then you merge them to print the completed letters.

1 Create a primary file.

Press	↵ENTER six times	Inserts blank lines before date.

You can insert the current date as text or as a code. When you insert it as a code, the letter is always printed with the current date using the computer's clock.

Select	"Tools," "Date Code"	Inserts date as code.

You can execute the Date Code command from the keyboard with the Shift-F5 key.

Press	↵ENTER five times	Inserts blank lines before address.
Select	"Tools," "Merge Codes"	Displays Merge Codes menu.
Select	"Field"	Displays "Enter Field."
Type	1	Numbers name field.
Press	↵ENTER	Displays {FIELD}1~.

A tilde (~) marks the end of each field. It is entered automatically with the merge code. You can execute the Merge Codes command from the keyboard with the Shift-F9 key.

Press	F11	Displays [Mrg:FIELD] code.
Press	F11	Removes Codes screen.
Press	↵ ENTER	Moves cursor to next line.
Select	"Tools," "Merge Codes," "Field"	Displays "Enter Field."
Type	2	Numbers address field.
Press	↵ ENTER	Displays {FIELD}2~.
Press	↵ ENTER	Moves cursor to next line.
Select	"Tools," "Merge Codes," "Field"	Displays "Enter Field."
Type	3	Numbers city field.
Press	↵ ENTER	Displays {FIELD}3~.
Press	↵ ENTER twice	Inserts double space.
Type	Dear	Inserts beginning of salutation.
Press	SPACEBAR	Inserts a space.
Select	"Tools," "Merge Codes," "Field"	Displays "Enter Field."
Type	4	Numbers salutation field.
Press	↵ ENTER	Displays {FIELD}4~.
Type	:	Inserts colon after tilde.
Press	↵ ENTER twice	Inserts double space.

Type the following paragraphs to complete the letter.

```
Did you forget? The library books you checked out last
month are overdue. The fine is ${Field}5~ if you pay today.
It will increase a nickel a day. If you lost the book,
please stop at the front desk and we will tell you the cost
of the book.

You will not be permitted to check out any materials until
the fine is paid. Please take care of this matter as soon
as possible.

Sincerely,


Edward Annenberg
Circulation Director
```

TIP: It is helpful to use an extension for primary and secondary documents. "PF" represents primary file. "SF" denotes secondary file.

Select	"File," "Exit," "Yes"	Displays Save prompt.

Name this document using an extension. ◀

Type	topic19.pf	Enters filename with extension.
Press	↵ ENTER	Displays Exit prompt.
Select	"No"	Clears screen.

2 **Create a secondary file.** The screen should be clear.

Type	Mr. Carlos Mostek	Enters name for first field.
Select	"Tools," "Merge Codes," "More"	Displays Merge Commands window.

Merge commands are listed in alphabetical order. Highlight a command with the arrow keys or by typing the first letter.

Type	e	Highlights {ELSE}.
Press	↓	Highlights {END FIELD}.
Press	↵ ENTER	Inserts {END FIELD} code.

TIP: If you mistakenly press F9 in any document, you will see {END FIELD}. The code can be deleted, but you will still see the "Field" prompt in the lower left corner. To remove the prompt, press HOME, HOME, UP.

The code is placed at the end of the name, and the cursor moves to the next line.

Type	4701 South Grant Street	Enters address for second field.
Press	F9	Inserts {END FIELD} code.

The {END FIELD} command is probably the most often used command in a secondary file, so it has a keyboard shortcut, F9. ◀

Type	Fremont, CA 94555-4701	Enters city for third field.
Press	F9	Inserts {END FIELD} code.
Type	Mr. Mostek	Enters salutation for fourth field.
Press	F9	Inserts {END FIELD} code.
Type	1.25	Enters amount for fifth field.

The dollar sign ($) that will print with the fine ($1.25) is in the primary letter.

Press	F9	Inserts {END FIELD} code.

Select	"Tools," "Merge Codes"	Displays Merge Codes menu.
Select	"End Record"	Inserts {END RECORD} code.

The code and a hard page break are placed at the end of the first record.

Type	Mr. Jonathan Eastman	Enters name for first field.
Press	↵ENTER	Moves cursor to next line.

The company name is included in field 1.

Type	Star Enterprises	Enters company name for first field.
Press	F9	Inserts {END FIELD} code.
Type	312 East Blandens Parkway	Enters address for second field.
Press	F9	Inserts {END FIELD} code.
Type	Emeryville, CA 94608-3120	Enters city and state for third field.
Press	F9	Inserts {END FIELD} code.
Type	Mr. Eastman	Enters salutation for fourth field.
Press	F9	Inserts {END FIELD} code.
Type	1.05	Enters amount for fifth field.
Press	F9	Inserts {END FIELD} code.
Select	"Tools," "Merge Codes," "End Record"	Inserts code and page break.

Type the third record as shown here.

```
Ms. Mary Ellen Albrecht{END FIELD}
7924 South Wilshire Avenue{END FIELD}
Emeryville, CA 94608-7924{END FIELD}
Ms. Albrecht{END FIELD}
.75{END FIELD}
{END RECORD}
=======================================
```

Select	"File," "Exit," "Yes"	Displays Save prompt.
Type	topic19.sf	Enters filename with extension.
Press	↵ENTER	Displays Exit prompt.
Select	"No"	Clears screen.

> **TIP** If you name a file with an extension, you must include the extension when you type the name. You can use the List Files command when prompted for the primary or secondary filename and retrieve the file from there.

> **TIP** If you find errors in the letters, you need to determine if the error is in the primary file or in the secondary file. If an error appears in all the letters, check the primary file first. Errors are more commonly made in the secondary file.

3 **Merge print.** Make sure the screen is clear before starting any Merge Print.

Select	"Tools," "Merge"	Displays "Primary file."
Type	topic19.pf	Enters primary filename.
Press	↵ ENTER	Displays "Secondary file."
Type	topic19.sf	Enters secondary filename.
Press	↵ ENTER	Displays "Merging."

The two files are merged on the screen into three letters. The cursor is on the third letter on page 3. ◀

Press	PAGE UP	Displays previous page.

Look at all three letters in the document.

Select	"File," "Print," "Full Document"	Prints three letters.
Select	"File," "Exit"	Displays Save prompt.

Clear the screen without saving the merged letters.

Select	"No," "No"

You can execute the Merge command from the keyboard with the Control-F9 key. ◀

PROCEDURE SUMMARY

CREATING A PRIMARY FILE

Type the constant text for the letter.	(your input)
Insert a merge code for variable data.	
Activate the menu bar.	ALT-=
Select "Tools."	T
Select "Merge Codes."	R
Select "Field."	F
Type the field number.	(your input)
Accept the field number.	↵ ENTER

CREATING A SECONDARY FILE

Type the field.	(your input)
End the field.	F9
Activate the menu bar.	ALT-=
Select "Tools."	T
Select "Merge Codes."	R
Select "End Record."	E

PRINTING MERGE LETTERS

Start with a clear screen.	
Activate the menu bar.	ALT-=
Select "Tools."	T
Select "Merge."	M
Type the primary filename.	(your input)
Accept the filename.	↵ENTER
Type the secondary filename.	(your input)
Accept the filename.	↵ENTER

EXERCISES

19A Complete the following tasks:

1. Type the following primary document.

```
Today's Date

{FIELD}1~
{FIELD}2~
{FIELD}3~

Dear {FIELD}4~:

Your appointment with {FIELD}5~ is at {FIELD}6~ next
Wednesday.

This is our Annual Career Day, and many more companies will
be on campus conducting interviews. If you would like to
schedule another appointment, please call our office soon.

Sincerely,


Josephine Baum
Placement Advisor
```

2. Press ENTER six times to add hard returns before the date. Use the Date Code to insert the code for the current date.
3. Press ENTER five times after the date. Number the merge fields as shown.
4. Use Spell.
5. Save your primary document as EXER19A.PF. Print one copy and clear the screen. Merge codes do not print.

19B Complete the following tasks:

1. Type the following secondary document.

```
Mr. Geoffrey Goodwin{END FIELD]
14222 Hilltop Drive{END FIELD}
Charleston, SC 32145-4222{END FIELD}
Geoffrey{END FIELD}
Global Electronics{END FIELD}
10 a.m.{END FIELD}
{END RECORD}
=====================================
Ms. Hillary Estevez{END FIELD}
Grinnell Hall
555 Lakeside{END FIELD}
Charleston, SC 32145-5552{END FIELD}
Hillary{END FIELD}
Star Computers{END FIELD}
12 noon{END FIELD}
{END RECORD}
=====================================
Mr. Thomas Fong{END FIELD}
107 East Plaza Way{END FIELD}
Columbia, SC 32148-1070{END FIELD}
Tom{END FIELD}
Star Computers{END FIELD}
11 a.m.{END FIELD}
{END RECORD}
=====================================
```

2. Save your secondary file as EXER19B.SF. Clear the screen.
3. Merge EXER19A.PF with EXER19B.SF and print the letters. Clear the screen after the letters are printed and do not save the merged letters.

Printing Envelopes

CONCEPTS

To type an envelope, you need to change the top and side margins to position the address in the correct location. Some word processors have an envelope selection that does all the work for you, including setting the margins, adjusting the paper size, and copying the address from the letter. All you need to do is insert the envelope at the printer.

Preparing an Envelope

When you select Envelope as the paper size in WordPerfect, the page dimensions are set at 9.5 × 4 inches, the standard business envelope size. Then you can set margins for an envelope and save the settings as a file. This file might be considered a "template," a basic format or design with text and/or codes. A "template" is used repeatedly without resaving. For an envelope, the template information is the margins and the envelope size.

Printing an Envelope

(168)

Whenever you need to type an envelope, retrieve the template file and type the address. Do not resave the file. If you do, the envelope template would include someone's address.

Some word processors have an automatic envelope procedure to copy the inside address from the letter to the envelope document. In WordPerfect, you use a second window to copy the address lines. By copying the address from the letter to the envelope, you are assured of accuracy.

To print an envelope, you need to determine how your printer handles the paper. Most printers require a simple adjustment for feeding the envelope.

Preparing a Merge Envelope File

After merge printing letters, you need envelopes for the letters, and the address information is in the secondary file. Merge envelopes follow a merge procedure like the letter. You create a new primary file, which includes margin and paper size formatting for a regular envelope. In this envelope primary file, you need to include Merge commands to extract the fields from the address list. An envelope primary file includes the same fields as the inside address of the primary letter.

Printing Merge Envelopes

Regular merge steps are used to combine the envelope primary document with the secondary file. The resulting document is a multipage document like the merged letters, but each page is an envelope.

To print multiple envelopes, you need to determine how to feed them through your printer. Most printers can be set to stop between each envelope and wait for you to insert the next one. This is "manual feed." On a laser printer, you can use the front panel to change to manual feed; the same is true for most dot matrix printers.

TUTORIAL In this tutorial, you create an envelope file and use it to address an envelope. Then you create an envelope primary file and use it to prepare envelopes for one of your merge letters.

1 Create an envelope file.

Select	"Layout," "Page," "Paper Size"	Displays Paper Size/Type menu.

The menu displays paper sizes available for your printer.

Select	"Envelope - Wide"	Displays Page Format menu.

The new Paper/Size type is displayed. An envelope is "wide" because the width is greater than the height.

Select	"Margins"	Moves cursor to top margin field.
Type	2	Enters new top margin.
Press	↵ENTER	Moves cursor to bottom margin field.
Press	↵ENTER	Accepts margins.
Press	↵ENTER	Displays Format menu.

You normally do not see this menu when you select "Line" or "Page" from the Layout menu.

Select	"Line," "Margins"	Moves cursor to left margin field.
Type	4.5	Enters new left margin.
Press	↵ENTER	Moves cursor to right margin field.
Press	↵ENTER	Accepts margins.
Press	F7	Returns to document.
Press	F11	Displays Codes screen.

The codes to position text on an envelope are shown in Figure 20.1. Standard margins for a business envelope are a 2-inch top margin and a 4.5-inch left margin. The bottom and right margins can be left at 1 inch.

Figure 20.1
Codes Screen for ENV

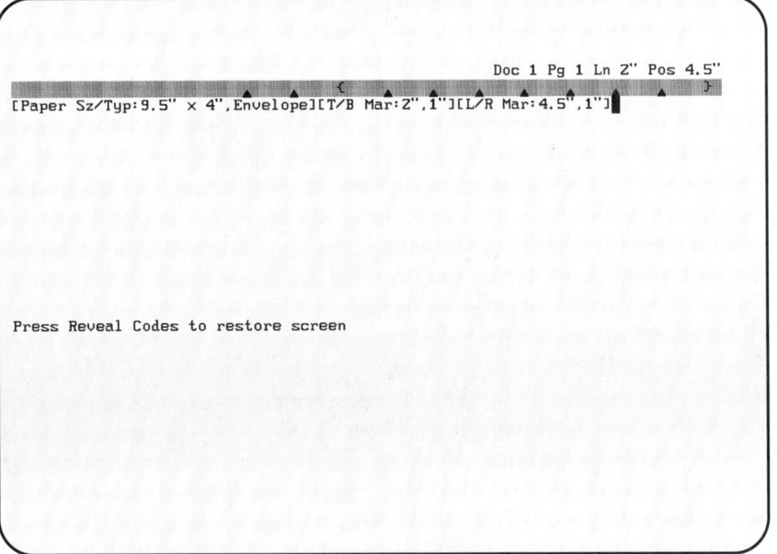

Press	(F11)	Removes Codes screen.
Select	"File," "Save," "Yes"	Displays Save prompt.
Type	env (↵ ENTER)	Saves ENV.

Address an envelope to yourself. Type your name, street address, and city, state, and ZIP on three lines. Prepare your printer to feed an envelope.

Select	"File," "Print," "Page"	Prints envelope.
Select	"File," "Exit," "No," "No"	Clears screen.

2 **Switch documents and copy an address.** Retrieve EXER12B from your disk.

Select	"Edit," "Switch Document"	Moves cursor to Doc 2.

The status line shows "Doc 2." There is nothing in Doc 2.

Select	"File," "Retrieve"	Displays Retrieve prompt.
Type	env (↵ ENTER)	Retrieves ENV in Doc 2.
Select	"Edit," "Switch Document"	Displays letter in Doc 1.

Watch the screen to position the cursor on the first character of the inside address.

Press	↓	Moves cursor to first address line.
Select	"Edit," "Block"	Displays "Block on."
Press	↓ three times	Highlights three address lines.
Press	CTRL-INSERT	Displays Retrieve prompt.

If you have a standard keyboard, select "Edit," "Copy" rather than pressing Control-Insert.

Select	"Edit," "Switch Document"	Moves cursor to Doc 2.
Press	↵ ENTER	Copies address to Doc 2.
Press	F11	Displays codes before address.
Press	F11	Removes Codes screen.

Prepare your printer to feed an envelope.

Select	"File," "Print," "Page"	Prints envelope.
Select	"File," "Exit," "No"	Displays "Exit Doc 2?"
Select	"Yes"	Returns cursor to Doc 1.
Select	"File," "Exit," "No," "No"	Clears screen.

3 **Prepare a merge envelope file.** Retrieve TOPIC19.PF from your disk.

Select	"Edit," "Switch Document"	Moves cursor to Doc 2.
Select	"File," "Retrieve"	Displays Retrieve prompt.
Type	env ↵ ENTER	Retrieves ENV in Doc 2.
Select	"Edit," "Switch Document"	Displays letter in Doc 1.

Watch the screen to position the cursor on the left brace with {FIELD}1~ in the address.

Press	↓	Moves cursor {FIELD}1~.
Select	"Edit," "Block"	Displays "Block on."
Press	↓ three times	Highlights merge codes.
Press	CTRL-INSERT	Displays Retrieve prompt.
Select	"Edit," "Switch Document"	Moves cursor to Doc 2.

Pos 4.5" shows that the merge codes will be after the format codes. ◀

TIP You can use different primary files with a secondary file. You might, for example, have a letter, an invoice, a phone list, a table, and a contract that use the same secondary document. Make sure the primary field numbers are in the order to extract information from the secondary file as necessary.

Press	↵ ENTER	Copies codes to Doc 2.
Press	F11	Displays Codes screen.
Press	F11	Removes Codes screen.
Select	"File," "Exit," "Yes"	Displays Save prompt.
Type	envmerge	Enters filename.
Press	↵ ENTER	Displays "Exit Doc 2?"
Select	"Yes"	Returns cursor to Doc 1.
Select	"File," "Exit," "No," "No"	Clears screen.

Figure 20.2
ENVMERGE File

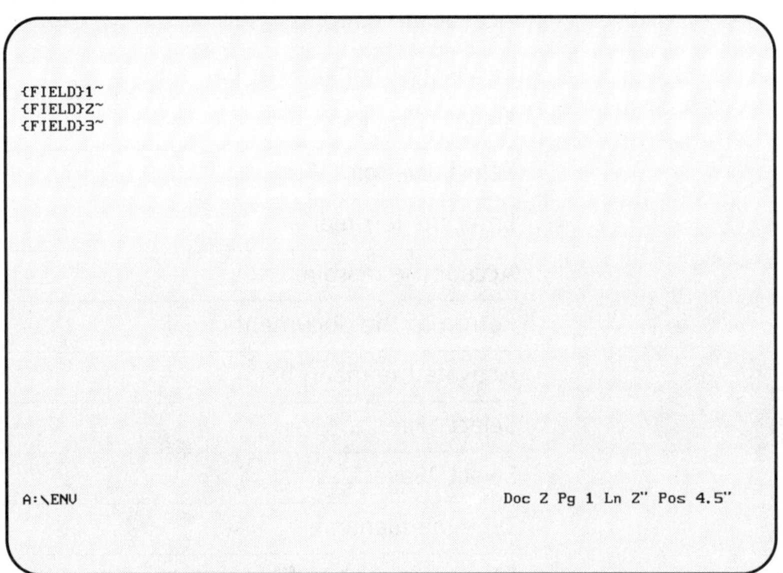

4 **Merge print the envelopes.** The screen should be clear.

Select	"Tools," "Merge"	Displays "Primary file."
Type	envmerge	Enters primary filename.
Press	↵ ENTER	Displays "Secondary file."
Type	topic19.sf	Enters secondary filename.
Press	↵ ENTER	Merges envelopes on screen.

Prepare your printer to feed three envelopes. You may need to print by "Page" depending on your printer.

Select	"File," "Print," "Full Document"	Prints envelopes.
Select	"File," "Exit," "No," "No"	Clears screen.

PROCEDURE SUMMARY

PREPARING AN ENVELOPE

Activate the menu bar.	ALT-=
Select "Layout," "Page."	L, P
Select "Paper Size."	S or 7
Select "Envelope - Wide."	(your input)
Accept the paper size/type.	S or 1
Select "Margins."	M or 5
Enter the top margin.	2
Accept the margins.	↵ENTER twice
Return to the main Format menu.	↵ENTER
Select "Line Format."	L or 1
Select "Margins."	M or 7
Enter the left margin.	4.5
Accept the margins.	↵ENTER twice
Return to the document.	F7
Activate the menu bar.	ALT-=
Select "File."	F
Select "Save."	S
Type the filename.	(your input)
Save the envelope file.	↵ENTER

PRINTING AN ENVELOPE

Retrieve the ENV file if necessary.	
Activate the menu bar.	ALT-=
Select "File."	F
Select "Retrieve."	R
Type the filename.	(your input)
Retrieve the file.	↵ENTER
Type the name and address for the envelope.	(your input)
Activate the menu bar.	ALT-=
Select "File," "Print."	F, P

Select "Page."	P or 2
Clear the screen without resaving the ENV file.	
Activate the menu bar.	ALT-=
Select "File."	F
Select "Exit."	X
Select "No" twice.	N twice

PREPARING A MERGE ENVELOPE FILE

Change the paper size/type.	
Activate the menu bar.	ALT-=
Select "Layout."	L
Select "Page."	P
Select "Paper Size."	S or 7
Select "Envelope - Wide."	(your input)
Accept the paper size/type.	S or 1
Select "Margins."	M or 5
Enter the top margin.	2
Accept the margins.	↵ ENTER twice
Return to the main Format menu.	↵ ENTER
Select "Line Format."	L or 1
Select "Margins."	M or 7
Enter the left margin.	4.5
Accept the margins.	↵ ENTER twice
Return to the document.	F7
Activate the menu bar.	ALT-=
Select "Tools."	T
Select "Merge Codes."	R
Select "Field."	F
Type the field number.	(your input)
Enter the next field code on a new line.	↵ ENTER
Activate the menu bar.	ALT-=
Select "File," "Exit."	F, X

Save the file.	Y
Enter the filename.	(your input)
Accept the filename.	↵ENTER
Clear the screen.	N

PRINTING MERGE ENVELOPES

Start with a clean screen.	
Activate the menu bar.	ALT-=
Select "Tools," "Merge."	T, M
Type the primary envelope filename.	(your input)
Accept the filename.	↵ENTER
Type the secondary filename.	(your input)
Accept the filename.	↵ENTER
Prepare your printer to feed multiple envelopes.	
Activate the menu bar.	ALT-=
Select "File," "Print."	F, P
Select "Full Document."	F or 1

EXERCISES

20A Complete the following tasks:

1. Retrieve CKPT1A.
2. Switch to Doc 2. Retrieve ENV into Doc 2.
3. Switch to Doc 1 and block/copy the inside address lines.
4. Switch to Doc 2 and retrieve the copied address block. Check the "Pos" number in the status line. Make sure the cursor is located after the codes before retrieving.
5. Print the envelope.
6. Clear both documents from the screen.

20B Complete the following tasks:

1. Retrieve EXER19B.SF. This secondary file has three address fields. You can use it with ENVMERGE to print envelopes.
2. Clear the screen.
3. Merge ENVMERGE with EXER19B.SF. Print the envelopes.
4. Clear the screen and do not save the merged envelopes.

Checkpoint 3

What You Should Know

- ✓ Pages are numbered as a document is typed, but the numbers print only after you give the Page Numbering command. You can position the printed number in several positions on the page as well as change the starting number.
- ✓ A header is text that appears at the top of every page; a footer appears at the bottom.
- ✓ A footnote is used to list a source of information or explain a concept in the text. The footnote appears at the bottom of the page with a superscripted number.
- ✓ Form letters are called merge documents. You need a primary file and a secondary file for completed letters. The primary file includes {FIELD} codes, which are numbered. The secondary file includes {END FIELD} and {END RECORD} codes.
- ✓ Files can be saved with extensions to help organize your work. Sample extensions are PF for primary files and SF for secondary files.
- ✓ Envelopes can be typed by changing the paper size/type to an envelope. Then you need to enter the top and left margins for an envelope. If you save the codes as a template file, you can retrieve the file to type envelopes.

Review Questions

1. What is the command to start page numbering?
2. What are three possible positions for page numbers?
3. How can you remove a footer?
4. How can you change the text in a header?
5. How is a footnote different from a footer?
6. What are the steps to delete a footnote?
7. What happens if you insert a footnote between Footnotes 2 and 3?
8. Describe the steps to create a primary file.
9. What command is used to mark the end of each piece of data in a secondary file?
10. What is each individual's set of information in a secondary file called?
11. What paper size/type is used for an envelope?
12. How can you copy the address from a letter to the envelope file?
13. What codes are needed to prepare a merge envelope primary file?
14. How do you feed an envelope through your printer?
15. How can you display the current date in a document?

CHECKPOINT PROBLEM A

1. Type the following report with page numbers, a header, and footnotes. Number the pages in the lower right corner.

MONOPOLY AND GLOBAL COMPETITION

American firms increasingly compete in international markets. Markets for stereos, VCRs, TVs, computers, and other goods are likely to include not only American but foreign manufacturers. The relevant market for a product also has a geographic aspect which concerns the area of effective competition.[1]

The relevant product market should include available substitutes as well as potential substitute products that would be produced if the price were raised. This concept recognizes that firms currently using assets to produce goods could easily convert to make substitutes for a monopolist's product.

For some goods, transportation costs, traditional sales areas, the perishable nature of the goods and other factors limit the scope of competition and create a regional market. For example, a surgeon or primary care hospital in Santa Fe, New Mexico, may provide the same services as surgeons and hospitals in Charleston, South Carolina. The Santa Fe hospital is not, however, a reasonable substitute for injured persons in Charleston.[2]

Once the relevant market has been defined, the court can determine a firm's share of that market. Although a high market share is not proof of monopoly power, it may be evidence from which monopoly power can be inferred. A low market share may preclude the need for further study, however. A 90 percent market share is surely enough to create power, but a 33 percent share is not clearly sufficient. Recent court decisions have suggested that a market share in excess of 50 percent may infer monopoly power.

Monopoly power does not exist, however, unless some barrier prevents other firms from entering the market if the dominant firm raises its prices. A barrier can be, but need not be, something created or caused by the dominant firm. Any market force that makes entry more costly or time consuming and reduces the effectiveness of potential competition should be considered a barrier.

[1]See United States vs. Carostein Steel company, 335 U.S. 495, 510-511 (1978).

[2]See Roth Storage & Van Company vs. Flash Van Lines, 792 F. 2d 210 (D.C. Circuit, 1986).

```
   Under economic theory, any characteristic of the market
that excludes or delays entry is a barrier to entry.
Possible barriers include the need to acquire expensive or
specialized plants or equipment, the need to obtain govern-
mental approvals through regulatory procedures, and the need
to overcome heavy brand promotion by existing companies.
```

2. Create a header to show the company name of "Echols, Hartman, & Smith." Use Flush Right to position the name at the right margin.
3. Suppress all page numbering, headers, and footers on the first page of the report.
4. Type the title using a large font. Triple space after the title and change to double spacing.
5. Enter the footnotes as illustrated.
6. Use Spell.
7. Save your work as CKPT3A.
8. View your work, make corrections, resave it if necessary, and print the document.

CHECKPOINT PROBLEM B

1. Prepare the memo primary file. Center the heading using a large font. Set a tab at +1". Use "Date Code" to enter the date.
2. Save the primary file as CKPT3B.PF.
3. Clear the screen and create the secondary file. The fields in the secondary file are not in the same order in which they are used in the primary file.
4. Save the secondary file as CKPT3B.SF.
5. Merge the memo and the employee list. Print the completed memos and clear the screen.

Primary File

MEMORANDUM

```
TO:        {FIELD}1~
           {FIELD}4~

FROM:      (Your Name)
           Human Resource Director

DATE:      Today

SUBJECT:   Information Update

Your personnel file shows that your current address is
{FIELD}2~, {FIELD}3~.

Your date of birth is {FIELD}6~. Your current beneficiary is
{FIELD}5~.

Please let us know if any information needs to be changed.
```

```
Secondary File

Miss Ruth Montague{END FIELD}
932 Cactus Lane{END FIELD}
Scottsdale, AZ 85011-2757{END FIELD}
321-45-9000{END FIELD}
Henri Montague{END FIELD}
May 8, 1967{END FIELD}
{END RECORD}
===========================================
Mr. Yan Tso{END FIELD}
909 West Grand Avenue{END FIELD}
Scottsdale, AZ 85011-9090{END FIELD}
000-22-0999{END FIELD}
Mary Tso{END FIELD}
July 4, 1959{END FIELD}
{END RECORD}
===========================================
```

COMPREHENSIVE EXERCISE

1. Set the top margin at 0.5 inch. Capitalize and center your name using a large, bold font. Return to your default base font after your name. The street address is left; the city, state, and zip is centered; the phone is flush right.
2. Type a primary letter using one field for the inside address and a second field for the salutation.
3. Before the listed items, set one tab at +0.75". Indent the listed items from both the left and the right margins.
4. Save the letter as RESUME.PF.
5. Use the Thesaurus to change the word "spotting" to an appropriate synonym.
6. Move the third listed item to make it the first item.
7. Replace all occurrences of "data processing" with "information systems."
8. Use Spell, proofread, resave the letter, and clear the screen.
9. In a secondary file, type the three names, addresses, and salutations. If you prefer, you can substitute companies you would like to write to. Save the file as COMPANY.SF.
10. Clear the screen. Merge the documents, view the pages, make any necessary corrections, and print the three letters.
11. Block your name and address on page 1. Include the top margin, bold, and font size codes in the block. Save the block as NAME-ADD.
12. Clear the screen without saving the merged letters.
13. Retrieve NAME-ADD. Set tabs at +1.75" and +2.25". Type the resume.
14. Press ENTER three times before each side heading. Use bold or italic for the side headings. Indent and bold the degree and the position names. The job responsibilities are indented two tabs.
15. Save the resume as DRAFT.RES. Block the page and append it to RESUME.PF. Clear the screen. List the files and rename RESUME.PF as RESUME.ALL.
16. Retrieve RESUME.ALL. Check the page break between the cover letter and the resume. Insert a hard page break if necessary so that the resume is on a separate page.
17. Start a new page at the end of RESUME.ALL. Retrieve NAME-ADD and type the follow-up letter to Land Enterprises.
18. Use Spell, proofread, resave, and print the resume and the follow-up letter.

ELLEN E. EASTMAN

5712 Central Avenue Louisville, KY 40220 (713) 869-3321

Current Date

{FIELD}1~

Dear {FIELD}2~:

Are you planning to strengthen the data processing in your company? My diverse data processing experience could be very beneficial to you. With my educational and PC background, I have assumed responsibilities and performed assignments not normally associated with my current position of student lab aid. For example:

I have trained students and staff to perform common DOS tasks and work with a myriad of software on a network; I have a knack for spotting errors in RPG, COBOL, and C programs.

I am proficient in using Novell's Netware including setting up new stations and modifying access rights.

I have assumed responsibilities for loading, maintaining, and trouble shooting 150 computers in the main PC lab.

My approach in fulfilling the duties of this position reflects my continued striving to acquire new knowledge and challenges. I am seeking a PC coordinator position in your data processing organization. I will assist you in meeting the demands of the 1990's with new, innovative data processing services. Enclosed is my resume for your review. I am looking forward to discussing a job opportunity with you.

Sincerely,

Ellen Eastman

Enclosure

```
Ms. Irene Snowden
Personnel Manager
Acme Financial Industries
175 West Jackson Boulevard
Pratt, KY 40321{END FIELD}
Ms. Snowden{END FIELD}
{END RECORD}
==============================================
Director of Data Processing
Banashire Steel Products
One Garden State Parkway
Denver, CO 80224{END FIELD}
Sir or Madam{END FIELD}
{END RECORD}
===========================================
Mr. Ryan Doherty, Director
Management Information Systems
Land Enterprises, Inc.
233 East Wacker Drive
Chicago, IL 60601{END FIELD}
Mr. Doherty{END FIELD}
{END RECORD}
=============================================
```

ELLEN E. EASTMAN

5712 Central Avenue Louisville, KY 40220 (713) 869-3321

Objective To work as a PC coordinator in a large company.

Education **Bachelor of Science**, Computer Science, Western Technology Institute, Houston, TX, 1991

Experience **Lab Aid**, Western Technology Institute, Houston, TX, 1988 to Present

Aided students and staff in lab.

Implemented a maintenance program for computers.

Assisted in networking classroom labs.

Intern, Reckitt & Midway, Inc., Rome, KY, Summer 1990

Network manager during vacation of network administrator.

Wrote WordPerfect macros for staff.

Achievements Outstanding Computer Science student, 1991.

Elected to the Computer Advisory Board by faculty and staff, 1990.

I have had five different PC tips published in national computer magazines.

References References are available from former employers, business associates, and professors upon request.

ELLEN E. EASTMAN

5712 Central Avenue   Louisville, KY 40220   (713) 869-3321

Current Date

Mr. Ryan Doherty, Director
Management Information Systems
Land Enterprises, Inc.
233 East Wacker Drive
Chicago, IL 60601

Dear Mr. Doherty:

Thank you for the opportunity of meeting you and your supervisors yesterday. I appreciated the time you shared with me discussing my career possibilities with Land Enterprises. It is apparent that Land Enterprises is on the cutting edge of technology; a place where I would like to work.

Your company will gain an experienced PC coordinator, a responsible person who wants to work, and a patient individual who will lead your employees to greater productivity utilizing their computer. I feel that with my experience, education, and background, I will be able to help you accomplish your goals. I'm enthusiastically looking forward to being part of your team.

Sincerely,

Ellen E. Eastman

Index

A

Aligning Text, 83

B

Blocks of Text, 67

C

Center Justification, 84
Copying text, 75
Current Directory
  checking the, 4, 7

E

Envelopes
  preparing, 163, 168
  preparing a merge envelope file, 163, 166-167, 169-170
  printing, 163, 168
  printing merge envelopes, 163, 167, 170

F

Files
  copying, 109-110, 113
  deleting, 109, 112-113
  finding, 110-111, 114
  managing, 109
  renaming, 109-110, 113
File management, 109
Footnotes
  creating a, 145-146, 150
  deleting, 145, 148-149
  editing, 145, 147-148, 151
  moving, 146, 149-151
  using, 145
Footers
  creating, 137, 142
  editing, 137, 141-143
  suppressing, 138, 140-141, 143
Form letters
  creating a primary file, 153, 155-157, 159
  creating a secondary file, 154, 157-158, 160
  preparing, 153
  printing merge letters, 155, 159-160

H

Hard Page Break, 120, 125-126
Headers
  creating, 137, 142
  editing, 137, 141-143
  suppressing, 138, 140-141, 143
Help facility
  using, 4

I

Indent command, 115

K

Keyboard Commands
  using, 4

M

Margins, 31
Menus
  using, 4, 7
Moving text, 75
Move command, 115

O

Orphan, 119

P

Page Breaks, 119-120
Page Numbers, 129
Printing, 25

S

Search command, 93-95, 115
Spell, 101
Spell program, 101

T

Tabs, 41-47
Template, 163
Thesaurus, 101

W

Widow, 119
Widow/orphan protection command, 119, 125
WordPerfect
  current directory, 4, 7-8
  exiting, 4, 8
  help facility, 4
  keyboard commands, 4
  menus, 4, 7
  screen, 3-4
  starting, 3, 7
WordPerfect Document
  aligning text, 83
  appending text in a, 75, 79-81
  blocks of text , 67
  canceling a print job, 26, 28-29
  center justification, 84
  centering text horizontally in a, 83, 85-86, 90
  centering text vertically in a, 83, 86, 90
  changing margins in a, 31, 37, 39
  changing tabs in a, 41, 44-45, 47
  changing the line spacing in a, 49-51, 53
  changing the page number in a, 129, 131-132, 134
  changing the paper orientation in a, 49, 51-53
  checking spelling in a, 101-105, 107
  choosing a page number position, 129, 134
  clearing the screen in a, 10, 12-13
  copying text in a, 75, 78-80
  creating a footnote in a, 145-146, 150
  creating a header or footer in a, 137, 142
  defining a block of text in a, 67, 72
  deleting a block of text in a, 67, 69, 72
  deleting a code in a, 32, 34, 39
  deleting a footnote in a, 145, 148-149, 151
  deleting text in a, 16, 19, 22
  editing a footnote in a, 145, 147-148, 151
  editing a header or footer in a, 137, 141-142
  inserting a code in a, 32, 34, 39
  inserting text in a, 15, 18, 22
  justifying text in a, 83, 87, 90-91
  keeping lines together on a page in a, 119, 126
  listing files, 15, 22
  moving a footnote in a, 146, 149-151
  moving text in a, 75-78, 80
  moving the cursor in a, 9, 13
  placing page breaks in a, 119
  previewing a, 25-26, 29
  printing a block of text in a, 68, 73

printing a page within a, 25, 27, 29
printing from the list, 25, 27, 29
printing, 25
resaving a file, 16, 21, 23
retrieving a file, 15-17, 21-22
right-aligning text in a, 84, 88, 91
saving a block of text in a, 67, 69-70, 72
saving the document, 10, 12-13
searching and replacing text in a, 93, 96-97, 99
searching for text or codes in a, 93-97, 98-99
setting left and right margins in a, 31, 38
setting tabs in a, 41, 46
setting top and bottom margins in a, 31, 38-39
starting page numbers, 129-130, 133
stopping the page numbers, 130, 134
suppressing a header or footer, 138, 140-143
typing text in a, 9, 13
undeleting text in a, 19-20, 22
using a hard page break in a, 120, 125-126
using different tab types in a, 41, 47
using fonts in a, 60, 63-66
using indents in a, 84, 88-91
using italic or other styles in a, 59, 62-63, 65
using soft page breaks in a, 119, 122-123, 126
using the thesaurus in a, 102, 105-107
using underline or bold in a, 59-63, 65
using widow/orphan protection, 119-124, 126